I0815192

THE AVANT GARDENS

VISIONARIES AND GARDENS BEYOND WILD EXPECTATIONS

gestalten

GARDENS THAT CONNECT US

INTRODUCTION

I have been a gardener for as long as I can remember. It has at various points been an inspiration, a vocation, and a salvation. Spending so much time in the garden gives one a different perspective on things. You are slowed down, and you become more observant of the world around you, and your place within the ecosystem of life. As many gardeners will agree, gardening is a meditative process, one that can transport you into completely different frames of mind. But it wasn't until very recently, when I encountered something that Gilles Clément said, that my understanding of my own experiences in the garden truly crystallized. In his book *The Planetary Garden,* Clément states: "The 'planetary garden' is a means of living in harmony with nature, appreciating the ecosystem in all its diversity, acting as gardener and guardian." It has taken me many years to arrive at a similar conclusion: that to be a gardener is to interact with a living world of plants and nature. The relationship between a gardener and the natural world is one that develops in real time, responding and reacting to the elemental processes of the earth.

This may sound obvious, but as you will notice throughout this book, there's a very specific taxonomy of horticultural professionals: from gardener to garden designer, landscape designer, and landscape architect. I have even listed them here in the order that, to me, growing up, seemed like the hierarchy of things. If the gardener works with the living elements, the garden designer and landscape architect work with the concrete, and the physical architecture of a space. They are still engaged with the living elements too, but their focus is more on this structure. The preceding term of "garden" or "landscape" refers, in my mind, to the scale of the projects; generally, these words refer to something more domestic in scale. Early in my career, when people asked what I did, I would reply, "I'm a gardener." This would nearly always be met with an "elevation" in their response: "Oh, so you're a garden designer?" It seemed somehow that being a gardener was never enough.

We live in a society where status is conferred on roles, deemed more powerful, or more glamorous. Our veneration of designers fits in with our wider cult of celebrity. Yes, someone needs the vision and foresight to create something—and undoubtedly there are incredibly talented designers at work—but the thing we so often forget with gardens and landscapes is that they are constantly changing. Like so many elements of life, they endlessly evolve—and without gardeners, none of these schemes would be realized, or continue to exist. A garden is never finished, it is never static, and it is always a conversation with nature. As anyone who has ever planned and created a garden knows, the experience is all about learning. What you imagined may not always work, and what was never imagined may turn out to be the best thing of all.

During the pandemic, there was a lot of time to think—and like many people, I found myself reassessing many things. What was the garden, and what was its point? For me, it was apparent that so much of gardening had become a battle with nature, and an obsession with control. The time-worn language of real estate agents and television makeover programs portray the garden essentially as an "outdoor room." This has, in my experience, led to the garden being regarded in much the same way as interiors, with focus placed on making it tidy and clean. The garden has become a sanitized space, where there is an aversion to letting things be; when the leaves drop, we rush out to clean up the "mess."

Within the construct of ownership, we believe that a garden's boundaries indicate what's ours. But the garden is part of something much larger—it is still tapped into the natural world, open to the elements, and to the creatures that live among us. It's part of a world that doesn't observe the freehold. From the ecosystems in the soil beneath and the sky above, the garden is alive. It is with this in mind that I think we must change, and do so far more quickly than we have up until this point. Like every aspect of the way we live, the garden needs to be reconsidered in light of the environmental crises we face. The garden holds immense potential as a vehicle for reconnection, and for better understanding of the natural world. Even the smallest spaces can offer the chance to tap into these natural rhythms. So much of gardening is about observation: taking the time to actually look at the world around you, at what you are living amongst, and how you fit into that.

In this sense, the garden is actually the sum of all life within it. The greater the richness and diversity that can be supported in that space, the more fulfilling it can be. We need to really see the garden as an ecosystem, a microcosm of the macrocosm—one where all can be welcomed. This idea calls to mind the words of the great gardener Henk Gerritsen:

> My garden must never degenerate into a battle against nature. If that happens, or threatens to happen, I'm doing something wrong. Plants that can't live without the use of chemical fertilizers or pesticides don't belong in my garden. Not in any garden by the way; you have a garden for the fun of it. A garden is art, or a hobby, if you like, but not a matter of life or death.

As many of the gardens in this book testify, the thinking around gardens and landscape is fluid; the way we understand and read these spaces shifts. The idea of a wild garden isn't new, but it takes time for ideas to spread, and for people to see things differently. In recent years, these ideas have flourished; questions and conversations about what a garden can be in the midst of an ecological crisis have developed rapidly. The garden—and our understanding of it—is evolving. Within these pages you will find spaces that champion these ideals, that have fundamentally shifted the relationship between the garden and the landscapes that surround them. You will discover the first gardens designed with these principles in mind, see many examples of how the design and philosophy of this movement has developed, and be taken right up to the most recent and cutting-edge examples of wild and natural gardening.

My belief is that the garden is all about connection. It's about connecting to a place in the immediate physical sense, and in the widest cosmological sense. In this book we have tried to highlight a number of gardens that speak to this connection. These places show the endless and beautiful interpretations of finding these ideas, manifested in a variety of ways. From the English countryside, to the wooded valleys of the east coast of the United States, and the lush, tropical vegetation of Brazil, each one of these projects shares a commonality and a uniqueness. They all respond to where they are locally, and share an understanding of the same principles. Each place is a part of a bigger picture, and acts as a response to our most fundamental questions about what it means to connect with nature.

Many of these spaces speak to Clément's idea of the planetary garden. The call to live in harmony with nature and work with the land is one that connects all gardeners—whether we choose to respond to that call is another matter entirely.

It is clear to me now that the role of a gardener is far more important than I previously believed. I hope the crucial nature of this role comes across in this book, and that it inspires you to question your own relationship with the garden. If you leave this book having learned one thing, I hope it is this: to be in the garden is to be connected to something much bigger.

—John Tebbs

THE GARDEN OF A VICTORIAN VISIONARY

The Gardens at Gravetye represent a major shift in the 19th century toward an appreciation for a more natural style. Hugely influential at the time, the impact of this garden still resonates today.

Born in Ireland, William Robinson trained as a gardener before emigrating to London—by the 1860s, he was working at the gardens in Regent's Park. It was shortly after this that he began his career in garden writing. It was through writing that Robinson made his fortune; and in 1884, he bought the Manor at Gravetye. The following year, he set about creating what was to become a visionary garden.

Robinson was incredibly prolific, producing some of the most influential garden books of his time. Perhaps his most well-known work is *The Wild Garden,* which was considered groundbreaking when it was published in 1870. It championed the planting of hardy plants both native and exotic, in a naturalistic style that would mimic nature. It sparked a dialogue that reshaped how we think about gardens, one which continues to evolve today. Another of his books, *The English Flower Garden,* published in 1893, remains the best-selling garden book ever printed. Here, he encourages the reader to be individual in their approach to the garden, promoting the study of plants and how they interact with each other. Robinson's hope was that "each gardener's individual imagination and ability to create his own private, personal wilderness" would be awakened. Robinson also ran two of the most popular gardening journals of the day: *The Garden,* and *Garden Illustrated.* Truly, his influence on gardening cannot be overstated. At Gravetye, Robinson got to bring his many ideas to life. He experimented with the idea of a mixed border, where perennials, shrubs, and annuals would jostle for space.

Now under the stewardship of head gardener Tom Coward, the resulting borders continue to surprise and evolve. The meadows provide flowering interest from the snowdrops in February until the native wildflowers end in September. These meadows are a key feature of Gravetye—so much so, Robinson devoted an entire chapter of *The Wild Garden* to them. The estate also boasts orchards and experimental forestry. Robinson had a great love of trees, and planted many—including selections from his travels in the U.S., where he visited the environmental philosopher John Muir, a fellow champion of nature. Toward the end of his life, he also became good friends with the renowned garden designer Gertrude Jykell, with whom he shared a similar vision and aesthetic. Robinson's love of nature was a source of inspiration, and drove his advocacy for a wilder, yet softer garden. This thinking went against prevailing Victorian ideals, but proved extremely popular, and sparked a revolution in gardening which continues to this day.

OPPOSITE, PP. 12 AND 13 A selection of summer flowering perennials and climbing rose in full bloom. **P. 8** Looking back at Gravetye Manor from within the mixed perennial borders. Once the home of garden writer William Robinson, the manor is now a hotel. **P. 10** Aerial shot over the lawns and long mixed borders with perennials in bloom. The more wild areas can be seen beyond, which highlight the garden's fade into nature.

A COLORFUL HORTICULTURAL HOTBED

The home of gardener and writer Christopher Lloyd, Great Dixter was a test bed and inspiration for his life's work in the garden. Fergus Garrett continues the story of experimentation and education in this ever-evolving garden.

The house at Great Dixter is made up of three buildings—the first was built in the mid-15th century. The second, a yeoman's house from Benenden (across the border in Kent), was built in the early 16th century and moved to Northiam at the suggestion of architect Edwin Lutyens in 1910. Lutyens made extra additions in 1912, which brought Dixter to its current form.

Lutyens was also responsible for the reworking of the garden, and much of his architectural language remains today. Strong structural elements of yew hedging run alongside reworked farm buildings incorporated into the scheme; for example the chicken coop, which has been turned into an open-sided loggia.

All this architecture provides a great framework for the voluptuous planting that spills out at every turn of the garden. Dixter is a garden of contrasts—Lloyd's playful relationship with color saw him abandon conventions of good taste. Here, anything was possible, and clashing colors were positively encouraged. The garden became one of the most written-about spaces of the 20th century, thanks to Lloyd's almost 50 years of writing. During this time he produced 25 books, a weekly column in *Country Life* magazine that lasted for 42 years, and regular contributions to *The Guardian* and *The Observer*. His was a witty voice—sometimes acerbic, always authoritative—that offered an utterly unique perspective on the garden.

Fergus Garrett joined Lloyd as Head Gardener in 1993; theirs was a relationship that saw the garden evolve further in its unique philosophy. Garrett remains at the helm today, and the garden is managed in much the same way as in Lloyd's time: blending high-impact visual displays with a considered intimacy of combinations. With mixed borders of trees, shrubs, perennials, biennials, annuals, and climbers, the garden is "intensive but allowed to look comfortable," in Garrett's own words.

Wildflower meadows, inspired by William Robinson's gardens at nearby Gravetye, were initiated by Lloyd's mother Daisy, who was also an enthusiastic gardener and trailblazer. The meadows continue to flow into the garden at Dixter, bringing an ethereal sense of nature to the spot.

As a space for learning and nurturing the next generation, Dixter has flourished. In the words of the estate: "[as] one of the most dynamic and complex flower gardens in the world, we have a responsibility to pass on the skills needed to garden this way." Students come from around the world to learn in this setting. Each hopes a little bit of the Dixter magic rubs off on them, and can be transplanted far and wide.

OPPOSITE Displays of potted plants are delivered in a particularly Dixter style, mixing unexpected combinations and bold colors.

P.18 A view from the roof of Dixter, showing the topiary garden and pond and highlighting the interplay of contrasts. **P.20** The bird topiary provides a somewhat tongue-in-cheek structure to the softer palette of planting that surrounds it. **P.21** One of the many gardeners that work and train at Dixter.

ABOVE Rainwater collection from the shed roof and various cans of character for distributing it. **OPPOSITE** A handsome wall-trained fig tree covers one of Dixter's outbuildings. **P. 26** The long border with Great Dixter in the background. This border is at its peak from June to mid-August; Lloyd's aim was for it to look "exuberant and uncontrived."

A REPEAT PASSION IN MOROCCO

The Jardin Majorelle was a lifetime obsession for French artist Jacques Majorelle. After falling in love with Marrakesh, Majorelle purchased land there in 1923—and began to create his own unique world.

Over the following years, Majorelle built his house; in 1931, he added an atelier by the architect Paul Sinoir in the art deco style. After this, Majorelle began creating his own botanical garden in a former palm grove.

Vegetation in the garden can be classified into five categories: palms, bamboo, cacti, aquatic plants, and flowering potted plants. However, they were not grown in isolation from each other, as is the common approach in many botanical gardens. Instead, they are interspersed, creating layers of interest, textures, and forms. The garden was clearly another canvas for Majorelle, with the various plants serving as a palette of paints he used to create this oasis in the city. Two linear pools highlight the importance of water in Islamic garden design; they also create central planting axes within the garden. Both pools are edged by short walls painted Majorelle Blue, the intense shade Majorelle famously trademarked. It is seen throughout the site, linking both garden and buildings.

Throughout the 1930s and '40s the garden continued to evolve and grow, as Majorelle devoted much of his time to the project. But the costs of maintaining such a place were not cheap—so in 1947, the garden was opened to the public, with the goal of helping Majorelle with the upkeep. Sadly, Jacques Majorelle died following a car accident in 1962, and the garden fell into decline over the following years. In 1980, when the garden was threatened by development, fashion designer Yves Saint Laurent and his partner Pierre Bergé stepped in to rescue the garden and restore it to its former glory.

The garden now extends over 2.5 acres (1 hectare), and hosts over 300 species of plants from five continents. It offers a green oasis in the heart of the bustling city; hidden behind high walls is a magical garden that appeals to the senses and continues to inspire. Since 2010, it has been run by the non-profit Fondation Jardin Majorelle, with Bergé having served as director until his death in 2017. The garden attracts 700,000 visitors annually and remains one of Marrakesh's most alluring spots.

ABOVE AND OPPOSITE Collections of cacti and succulents create strong sculptural forms throughout the garden. **P. 28** The house is framed by palms and potted plants. The whole place emanates a compelling and consistent creative vision.

ABOVE The atelier designed by Paul Sinoir and painted in Majorelle's trademark shade of blue, with tall cacti echoing the bold architectural lines.

ABOVE Water is fundamental to Islamic garden design, and two linear pools in the garden reference this connection. **OPPOSITE** Aloe species in full bloom.

A GARDEN ACROSS GENERATIONS

On the east coast of Scotland, the Erskine family have called Cambo home for over 300 years. The garden is layered with history, but two women in particular have had a profound impact on its current appeal.

Peter and Catherine Erskine inherited the estate in 1976. Peter, a farmer, went on to found the Scottish Organic Producers Association. Catherine's love of gardening led to some impactful shifts within the garden. In 2001, she employed a new head gardener: Elliott Forsyth. It was a partnership that saw the development of quite an experimental approach—especially for the early 2000s.

Forsyth was keenly interested in the new naturalistic grass and perennial movement, and the work of Piet Oudolf in particular. He had visited Oudolf's garden at Hummelo in The Netherlands, as well as other examples of his work in the rest of Europe. This would ultimately serve as inspiration for what was created in the unique walled garden at Cambo. Unlike the typical walled garden of an estate, this one developed a much more natural feel, with soft, shaggy edges enhanced by a welcoming approach to certain self-seeders. The walled garden at Cambo provides a mixture of traditional elements like box hedges, roses, fruits, and vegetables, but also blends in areas of grasses and perennial planting. There is great skill in the mixture of form, texture, and color here, and its dispersal into unexpected areas such as the vegetables. The space definitely lies in the tradition of the New Perennial movement, but also produces an effect totally unique to Cambo. Forsyth's work also added a more timeless quality to the overall garden, extending its appeal late into the season. The importance of this cannot be overstated, as the estate generates much of its income as a visitor attraction.

Peter's grandmother Lady Magdalen Erskine, herself an avid gardener, provided the means for another key attraction of the gardens. Beginning in the 1930s, she and her eight children spent hours each year digging, dividing, and replanting snowdrops in the 70 acres (28 hectares) of woodland. So extensive was their work that by the 1980s, acres of woodland were covered in snowdrops, right down to the nearby sea. Realizing its potential, in 1986 Lady Erskine set up a mail-order snowdrop business and put up a sign advertising the woodland display. Snowdrop tourism wasn't much of a thing then, but it has grown to become quite a seasonal celebration around the country. People now regularly congregate outside to witness this mesmerizing display of winter drawing to a close for another year. Cambo now holds the Plant Heritage national collection of snowdrops, with over 200 varieties alongside the thousands of *Galanthus nivalis* at home in the Cambo woodlands.

It surely goes to highlight the garden's potential as a conduit for giving to future generations.

ABOVE Entrance to the walled garden of Cambo House. **PP. 36 AND 38** Inside, the garden has an unusual mixture of planting for a traditional-period walled garden. Previous head gardener Elliott Forsyth was inspired by the perennial planting style of the Dutch plantsman Piet Oudolf. A mixture of grasses, perennials, and fruit, and vegetables fill the beds. **P. 43** Traditional elements such as the glasshouses remain inside this interesting mix.

A POEM OF A GARDEN

The creation of writer Vita Sackville-West and her diplomat husband Harold Nicholson, Sissinghurst is one of those cult gardens that lives in the imagination as much as it does in the real world.

When the couple first visited Sissinghurst, the home was in a state of dereliction. It was being used to house farmworkers, and the grounds were scattered with rusty bedframes and old sardine tins. Still, Sackville-West said of her visit that she "fell in love; love at first sight. I saw what might be made of it. It was Sleeping Beauty's Castle."

Above all, Sissinghurst emerged out of romance. Both keen gardeners, Sackville-West and Nicholson brought themselves to the garden. Nicholson provided the architectural structure and framework: a series of rooms that Sackville-West then filled with her passion for plants. Roses were one of her favorites, as were flower beds bursting with color.

Sackville-West gardened instinctively, a great observer of things. This translated into her writing; in 1926, her poem "The Land" won the Hawthornden Prize. It celebrated her native Kent: its landscapes, rituals, dialects, and farming language. While at Sissinghurst, she turned her attention to the garden, both physically and in her writing. In 1946, she published her poetry collection "The Garden." Set against the backdrop of war, it follows the seasons of the garden, a metaphor for the seasons of life. Sackville-West mixed with the literary Bloomsbury set: she and her husband both had same-sex relationships throughout their marriage, and Sackville-West had a long connection with the novelist Virginia Woolf. In the 1920s, Sackville-West also wrote about her earlier relationship with Violet Keppel in *Portrait of a Marriage*, but it was not published until 1973, after her death.

In 1947, Sackville-West began a weekly column for *The Observer* newspaper, which she would continue for the rest of her life, making Sissinghurst one of the most well-known gardens in the country. Despite having no formal horticultural training, she had learned a great deal from her previous garden Long Barn, also in Kent. Experimentation and trial and error there stood her in good stead for Sissinghurst. Her innovation with single-plant gardens became her trademark, the White Garden being perhaps the most well-known example of this. Her series of garden rooms created a journey that captivated and transported the viewer from one scene to the next—from rose, to cottage, to orchard garden, and beyond.

Sackville-West was one of the founding members of the National Trust's garden committee in 1948, and Sissinghurst passed into its care when she died in 1962. It remains an outstanding testament to horticultural passion.

ABOVE AND P. 44 The Delos Garden by Dan Pearson is a recently completed (2021) reinterpretation of a part of Sissinghurst that was never quite finished by Sackville-West and Nicholson. Its lack of success was due to poor location and a lack of knowledge on Mediterranean planting. Drawing inspiration from a 1935 trip to the Greek island of Delos, the couple had hoped to recreate something of that back in Kent—nearly 90 years later, a true sense of the vegetation and landscape has been successfully distilled.

ABOVE, OPPOSITE, AND P.50 The White Garden at Sissinghurst is one of its most iconic elements. The use of variations on a single color was one of Sackville-West's trademarks, creating a dramatic planting impact. Its influence has led to it being a much-referenced feature in garden design.

ABOVE AND OPPOSITE Sackville-West and Nicholson each brought their own point of view to the gardens—soft and flowing planting with an eye for color inside a strong architectural framework was a hallmark of the partnership that created Sissinghurt.

LESS CULTIVATION, MORE OBSERVATION

If the garden is an engagement with nature within a boundary, then land art engages with a whole landscape without such boundaries.

Land art is an interaction with all the forces of nature: materials, elements, processes, and time. It fundamentally embraces the hand of nature in its creation, and in where it ends.

Making marks on the land is a process as old as time, a meeting point of everything understood and not understood, an expression of our relationship with nature. From the Nazca lines in modern-day Peru, to the Serpent Mounds of the Adena culture in present-day Ohio, to prehistoric hill carvings in England, history is filled with examples of us leaving our marks in and on the land.

The use of this concept in modern art came about in the 1960s and '70s, in the movement known as land art. Also sometimes referred to as Earth art or environmental art, this movement is hard to pin down in clear definitions. This was partly the point: this was art outside of the constructs of a gallery, where dealers were unable to put a price on the work, or shift its context with a rehang. This art was living and of a place; it was transient and mobile in its state. It was free, within and of the universe.

Land art of the 20th century emerged within the wider social narrative of the ecology movement. There were growing concerns about the way we were treating Earth; the relationship was already unsustainable and damaging, and was becoming abusive. Some people think of Earth art as being largely based in wild and dramatic landscapes. There are certainly many examples of this, but many artists also actively brought nature's processes into the city. These works serve as reminders of what was, could be, and no doubt will be again. Alan Sonfist's *Time Landscape* (proposed in 1965, and originally unveiled in 1978) brought the pre-colonial forest back to central New York. Located at the northeast corner of LaGuardia Place and West Houston Street, and several other locations across the city, *Time Landscape* consists of indigenous plants that once grew in the area, before they were buried under the sidewalks and skyscrapers of Manhattan. This evocative statement—part urban forest, part memorial—was and is a piece of land evolving, resonating something of the Earth to those who pass, reflecting back a memory from the subconscious.

A work which is more transient than Sonfist's but certainly no less powerful is Agnes Denes's *Wheatfield—A Confrontation* (1982). Denes set out to turn a 2-acre (8,100-square-meter) Battery Park landfill into a field of wheat. The site was cleared of garbage and then hand-sown, maintained, and harvested over four months, yielding more than 1,000 pounds (454 kilograms) of grain.

© Alfio Finocchiaro

ABOVE *A Line In* by British land artist Richard Long, 1981. **P.55** In 2015 Agnes Denes was invited to recreate her 1982 New York wheat installation in an urban area of new developments in Milan, Italy.

Growing wheat on land in central Manhattan valued then at 4.5 billion dollars (despite being a landfill), set between the Statue of Liberty in one direction and the Twin Towers and Wall Street in the other, asks so many questions about what we value in modern society.

Writing about her own work, Denes pointed out Manhattan's status as one of the wealthiest, most crowded pieces of land on the planet. Creating 2 acres (8,100 square meters) of wheat on such prime real estate was in fact a stand against the system. It was a paradox, something impossible and crazy, but in the same sense it grabbed people's attention highlighting the strange choices we make in prioritizing what is important. Denes articulated that Wheatfield was a symbol of a universal concept and one that, if ignored, would result in catastrophic consequences for humanity.

The striking images of this piece of land art taken at the time still resonate today. The sharp contrasts *Wheatfield* draws seem surreal but equally relevant 40 years on.

Of course, more land art was created outside of urban hubs in wild open landscapes. Robert Smithson's *Spiral Jetty* (1970), constructed at Rozel Point on the northeast shore of Great Salt Lake is a classic example. Monumental in its scale, *Spiral Jetty* was created using more than 6,000 tons (5,443 metric tons) of black basalt rock and earth from the location. These materials were wound into a counterclockwise coil from the shore into the lake. The work—at times covered by the lake, at times revealed, particularly during drought—is constantly evolving, responding to its environment. It became one of the most iconic artworks of its generation, but is equally timeless in its presence.

These examples suggest that land art was dominated by scale, but that was not the case. The somewhat more humble but equally moving work by Richard Long, *A Line Made by Walking* (1967), was created in a field in Wiltshire, England, where Long walked back and forth to create a line in the grass. He documented this with a photograph. The piece raised many questions: could walking be art? Is the artwork the act itself, the documentation, or both? Walking is an act of physical engagement with the earth; in many ways, the pathways we make through a landscape are some of the most powerfully timeless and most transient marks we make. This work took a simple everyday action and shone a light on its transcendental power.

Andy Goldsworthy's work was equally inspired by everyday experiences. Perhaps most well-known are his creations of walls and sculptures of delicately balanced stones, such as *Wall That Went for a Walk* (1989) in Grizedale Forest, Cumbria. The sculpture was inspired by his time spent working as a farm laborer in the north of England, where stone walls are an ancient man-made feature of the landscape. Monumental and stoic in the way they flow over and through the landscape, they appear as if they have grown out of the land. Like so many land artists, Goldsworthy works with a palette of materials found in the natural world: leaves, ice, pinecones, rocks, snow, earth, and stone. As Goldsworthy states: "Movement, change, light, growth, and decay are the life-blood of nature, the energies that I try to tap through my work."

Perhaps we are left wondering about the relationship between land art and the garden. The garden shares much with land art, working as it does with a palette of natural materials—living, moving, and changing constantly. At the end of the 20th and beginning of the 21st century, we have seen elements of the language of land art being incorporated into garden design. The mown path in the meadow is a constant feature we see in this book—of course, pathways have virtually always been a practical feature of the garden, but it is the visual language of land art that allows us to see the beauty in something as practical and seemingly mundane as a mown pathway. Prior to this artistic movement, we might not have acknowledged this as valid enough to focus on. Similarly, the stone wall has also gone from being purely a boundary marker to something possessing a sculptural power—worthy of incorporation in ways that go beyond its practical purpose.

Perhaps what we are witnessing in the garden is a shift in perspective. An appreciation of the framework—the pathways and boundaries—inevitably leads to a change of what is inside that framework. As our relationship with the garden evolves, maybe we will be better able to appreciate the ephemeral nature of the space, and question just how much control we really need to exert over it. Perhaps we'll be able to enjoy nature's processes in a way that derives more pleasure from simple observation.

"We often forget that *we are nature*. Nature is not something separate from us. So when we say that we have lost our connection to nature, we've lost our connection to ourselves."

Andy Goldsworthy

CELEBRATING AUSTRALIA'S UNIQUE FLORA

Colonial Australia has always had a dual relationship with the landscape it occupies. It was at once seen as awe-inspiring, and as something to be subdued, made to conform to European expectations of landscape.

In a former sand quarry, the largest botanic garden of Australian plants seeks to celebrate the natural flora of this landscape. It frames the narrative of the Australian landscape as a physical journey from desert to coast, led by the connecting element of water. There is, however, no prescribed path, and multiple routes offer a diversity of options that reflect the sheer scale of Australian ecosystems. It is a garden that seeks to inspire visitors to look at native flora with fresh eyes. It provides both stimulation and education on the diversity, beauty, and preservation of Australian flora.

Horticulturalist and designer Paul Thompson helped landscape practice T.C.L approach the challenging site of the former quarry. It had previously been left without soil and vegetation, forming a scar in the earth. Rather than importing soil, the team wanted to work with the existing site and with plants that could meet the challenge. Of course, much of Australia's native flora is familiar with extreme conditions, and well adapted to survive where other plants would fail. The site now includes 1,700 species, and some 170,000 plants, all adapted to the soil and climate conditions.

Located on the outskirts of the ever-expanding city of Melbourne, the garden is an important asset in a country particularly exposed to extreme climate events. Here, messages about sustainability and biodiversity are a key feature of the narrative, playing a vital role in helping not only the public but also scientists understand the past and future potential of Australia's incredible flora.

In a country that once looked to model itself on European ideals, the Australian Garden represents a dramatic shift. It connects to a wider change in approach and thinking about how to garden with native plants, and how to draw inspiration from Australia's natural landscapes and plant communities. In the words of the landscape practice T.C.L: "The garden highlights the tension between the natural landscape and our human impulse to steadily change it. This tension is not eliminated; rather it is the driving creative impulse for exploration, expression, and interpretation of the landscape and its flora."

ABOVE References to the site's former incarnation as a quarry echo aspects from Australia's diverse landscapes and reinterpret them into the garden.

P. 62 The Red Sand Garden is the centerpiece of the Royal Botanic Gardens—an artistic interpretation of the iconic red center at the core of Australia's geography. Circles of gray planting represent the vegetation dotted throughout this arid landscape. Surrounding this are a range of gardens which showcase other areas that encompass Australia's biodiversity.

ABOVE AND OPPOSITE Throughout the garden, paths lead in a myriad of ways, offering a host of possible routes, reflecting the sheer scale and diversity of Australian ecosystems. To let the visitor explore the many visions of Australia was part of this garden's conceptual approach.

LANDSCAPE, PLAYSCAPE: ALL IS SCULPTURE

A park project in Japan's northern city of Sapporo gave realization to many of Isamu Noguchi's long-held beliefs on landscape: its sculptural potential, and capacity to create a stimulating, playful experience.

Moerenuma Park was one of Noguchi's last projects and was completed after his death in 1988. It was in March of that same year that he first visited Sapporo, where the city had embarked on a "Circular Green Belt Concept" that would soon envelop the city in parks and green spaces. Work on the park had already begun in area that had been a landfill for the previous decade. However, this posed a positive opportunity for Noguchi, who in his words, could see the potential of "reviving the land damaged by humans through art."

Noguchi proposed the whole park should be conceived as a single sculpture. The project gave him the opportunity to realize many of his ideas around landscape and play. He had been deeply interested in exploring such ideas since the start of his career, but few commissions throughout his life had fully embraced this ethos, or offered Moerenuma's scale.

The park has many unique sculptural elements: mountain-like mounds, fountains, and over 100 unique playground pieces designed by Noguchi. Some of the main features within the park include Play Mountain, a 98-foot (30-meter) hill sculpted into the landscape, with 99 steps up one face and a gently sloping path down another. It is the realization of an idea Noguchi originally proposed in 1933 for New York's Central Park. Noguchi believed play should not be so prescriptive, leaving space for children to interact with space and form. He firmly believed that the way children experience play was fundamental to engage their imagination and creativity. The abstract nature of the sculptural elements of his playground pieces offer exactly this: a stark contrast to the rigidity of familiar homogenized playgrounds, which were—and are—so prevalent.

In front of Play Mountain is The Music Shell, which provides a stage for performances, bringing the landscape to life in other ways. Water provides another element of not only play, but also of sculpture through movement. The Aqua Plaza and Canal, Moere Beach, and Sea Fountain all offer different water-based engagements that provide ways to cool down in summer. In the case of Sea Mountain, this engagement takes the form of a dynamic water sculpture that expresses the birth and life of the universe, shooting water 98 feet (30 meters) into the air.

Moerenuma Park is a fascinating experiment in seeing the world through a different lens, where art and landscape come together to take us beyond the ordinary.

ABOVE Play Mountain, a 98-foot (30-meter) hill, was the realization of an idea Noguchi had proposed in 1933 for a playground in New York's Central Park that was never built.

P. 70 Water is a key element within the park. Set between Play Mountain and Mount Moere, the Aqua Plaza, a square of bubbling water and stone which flows into a shallow canal, is a great place to cool down in summer. **P. 76** The Music Shell provides a stage for musical performances and brings the park to life with sound—not on Noguchi's original plans, but resonates with his thoughts on music and play.

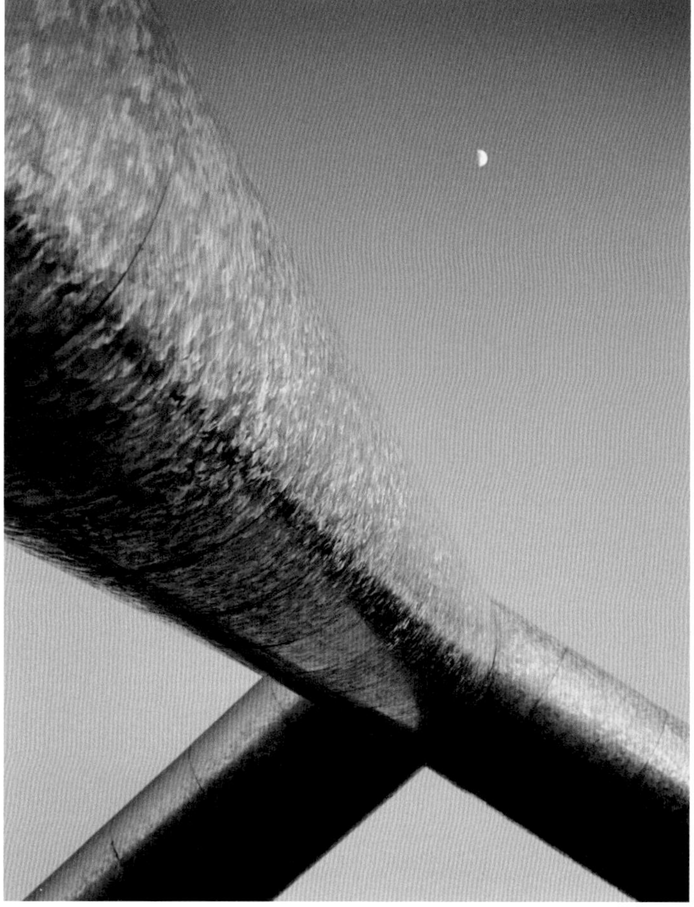

AN EVOLVING ARTWORK BEYOND THE GALLERY

When Hauser and Wirth opened a gallery at Dursdale Farm in rural Somerset, it seemed only fitting that Piet Oudolf—the master of sculptural, painterly planting—was asked to be involved.

Eponymously named, Oudolf Field is an ever-evolving masterpiece, and the largest of three gardens that surround the gallery space. The two smaller gardens are more subtle and contained in their language, leaving space to respond to the buildings. The Cloister Garden is aptly named, forming more of a meditative space. The planting—a sea of muted greens and browns featuring grasses and perennials—floats around the feet of a Louise Bourgeois spider, and gently moves in an endless dance with an Alexander Calder piece.

Away from this, you are drawn to the explosion of planting that lies in the neighboring field. This is known as Oudolf's signature work: grasses and perennials play out a performance throughout the year, demonstrating Oudolf's well-known belief that the garden should hold as much interest in winter as in summer. The beautiful seed heads and skeletal remains of the plants in winter provide a stark contrast to the colorful drifts and swaying grasses of high summer. This is a garden free from the pressure of being its "best" at any one time.

There is not a single prescriptive route through the garden. There are multiple options, and many diverging and winding paths. This means the viewer is free to explore and experience the meadow from as many angles as they choose. Indeed, it positively encourages you to take in as many of the dynamic planting compositions as possible, which deliver constantly shifting perspectives on the garden. Potential is lying around every turn. This garden is also a reminder that as an artwork, a garden is never truly the work of one person. Oudolf's composition is undeniably masterful, but how this space evolves is very much rooted in how its plants respond to conditions and seasons. This is a living, changing environment, and it reminds us that there is a huge element of letting go in a garden. We can control things to a certain extent, but there is much joy to be found in the unexpected results of time.

ABOVE Looking back at the Hauser and Wirth Somerset gallery buildings from Oudolf Field. **OPPOSITE TOP AND P. 78** Looking towards The Radić Pavilion, designed by Chilean architect Smiljan Radić. The structure arrived in 2015 after being commissioned for the Serpentine Gallery's annual pavilion in London in 2014.

OPPOSITE BOTTOM AND P. 80 Drifts of perennial planting—the work of Dutch maestro Piet Oudolf in the eponymously named Oudolf Field.

GARDEN RADICALS AND THE DUTCH WAVE

What constitutes "radical" in the world of gardening? New alliances between gardeners and nature; relationships that are observant, playful, and not held back by preconceived constructs.

The Netherlands is well-known for its strong connection to horticulture, both historically and in the present day. But in the 1970s, a tide of green counterculture emerged against what was happening in the Dutch landscape. The Netherlands was becoming one of the most industrially farmed countries in Europe; with the increasing popularity of fertilizers and pesticides, there was growing concern that the country's ecology would become sterilized by this explosion of big agriculture.

Henk Gerritsen was part of a group of gardeners, growers, and thinkers who were bouncing around ideas of what gardening was and could be. Seeing how much the natural landscape was becoming eroded, these thinkers proposed that gardening had to shift, and become more closely aligned with the rhythms of the natural world once more. As Gerritsen himself stated:

> Those who stick too rigidly to a pre-determined garden plan end up in a time-consuming battle with nature. Those who want gardening to remain an enjoyable endeavor have to be flexible. Change is not by definition wrong. Those who allow nature to take its course may witness fantastic results, so much so that it will surpass their wildest dreams.

Rob Leopold, Ton ter Linden, and Piet Oudolf—as well as a larger community of nature lovers, ecologists, photographers, and designers—were drawn into this conversation, forming what would later become known as the "Dutch Wave." Growers and nurserymen—often with a particular interest in perennial and native plants, seeds, and bulbs—also played a key role. In a horticultural system of increasingly homogenized plant offerings, these nurseries provided diversity and a different approach to the garden. The group did not have a manifesto, or an explicit goal—but they shared a common passion for plants, and for evolving the garden's relationship with nature.

Gerritsen's love of wildflowers saw him and his partner Anton Schlepers travel widely across Europe and beyond, observing plant communities growing in their natural habitats. In 1978, when Gerritsen and Schlepers set about creating Priona Gardens (considered their first garden), they called upon these interdependent plant communities for inspiration. In particular, Gerritsen cited the "awe inspiring flower meadows of Central and Southern Europe" as inspiration for what he hoped to achieve at Priona. Gerritsen aimed to create a garden that felt natural, and that also functioned naturally, without the need for chemicals, excessive

Piet Oudolf in the garden of his home at Hummelo.

Oudolf's signature perennial planting.

irrigation, or weeding. In nature, plants tend to find balance; they achieve success within an ecological equilibrium, and competition prevents any one particular species from becoming too dominant. The way they interrelate and grow together was what Gerritsen hoped to highlight in his own garden.

It was during his search for plants to grow in this style of garden that Gerritsen met many of the kindred spirits associated with the Dutch Wave. Gerritsen was looking for sturdy and robust plants not so far removed from their natural states (through plant breeding and hybridization), which could form a plant community, like the ones he observed in the wild. Such plants were found in abundance at Hummelo, a nursery run by Piet Oudolf and his wife Anja, which specialized in perennials and grasses. Oudolf had a strong interest in the English perennial garden: historically, a garden full of long borders that peaked in interest through the summer—often a heavily staked and stage-managed affair. He was keen to imagine a different perennial style, free from the rules of the English garden, and began to develop a different approach. He experimented with grasses and perennials in his own garden, initially planting in blocks or waves, echoing a more naturalistic style of design. This style was more fluid and flowing—a considered but seemingly wilder affair. The approach was successful; Oudolf became the name most associated with this style of gardening. He went on to receive a host of international and domestic commissions for private gardens and public spaces, including his two most famous works in North America: the Lurie Garden in Chicago, and the High Line in New York. Piet's planting style evolved over the years, shifting from something more aesthetically naturalistic to something that could be considered more ecological in its approach. This evolution perhaps highlights the cross-pollination of ideas that came about through the Dutch Wave. For Gerritsen, the ecology of a garden was more or less the starting point at Priona—as was reviewing outmoded perceptions of what a garden could be. As he stated in his essay on gardening:

A multitude of paths means there is no prescribed way to experience the planting. Each viewer is encouraged to find their own unique view.

> The idealized harmony of a symmetrical garden with straight hedges, an elongated straight pond in the middle and trees planted symmetrically on both sides (that never grow at the same speed: farewell symmetry), has outlived itself. It is a theme from the past, when people used to be afraid of nature, which was ubiquitous, and the fence of the garden was meant to lock nature out. Today, when nature around us has virtually disappeared, the chilly, nature-adverse surrounding has to be kept outside the fence. Logically the internal garden has to be landscaped in a different manner than it used to be, because nature is not symmetrical.

This reimagined relationship between nature and the garden was a crucial link in this narrative.

Another grower, friend, and fellow Dutch Wave figure that Gerritsen came into contact with was philosopher Rob Leopold. He owned Cruydt-Hoeck, a nursery established in 1978 that specialized in wildflower seeds. Leopold was attempting to save an abundance of native wild plants, which supported local ecosystems of butterflies, bees, and other meadow inhabitants. This biodiversity was being lost as industrial agriculture swept through the landscape, in a haze of heavy machinery and chemical sprays. As Gerritsen saw it, this attack on nature had no place in the garden:

> The maintenance of my garden must never degenerate into a battle against nature. If that happens, or threatens to happen, I'm doing something wrong. Plants that can't live without the use of chemical fertilizers or pesticides don't belong in my garden. Not in any garden by the way; you have a garden for the fun of it. A garden is art, or a hobby, if you like, but not a matter of life or death. Hence chemical fertilizers and pesticides, which are threatening the natural environment and consequently the health of all living creatures, ought to be forbidden for use in a garden.

Gerritsen's garden at Priona was an ever-evolving place, playful and deft in its interactions with nature. It was the birthplace of new ideas that challenged contemporary concepts of gardening, and reimagined what might be considered wild or natural in the garden space. At the heart of all these ideas was a celebration of nature: the way plants grow together, the biodiversity they host, and the idea that there is beauty throughout the cycle of life and death, in both success and failure. The Dutch Wave saw an appreciation of the garden year-round, particularly the perennial flower garden. The beauty of the transition from flower to seed head—from the gentle sway of the living stem, to the frozen architecture of the skeletal remains—is a poetic journey, and one to be embraced and witnessed. This in itself felt like a revolutionary thought at a time when gardeners were more familiar with the idea of tidy and manicured. As in nature, the seed heads in Priona stood through the winter, providing a completely changed perspective on the garden. This was about gardening in response to the conditions: the soil, the climate, and factors we cannot anticipate before we start digging. It was about playing with nature, rather than trying to play God with nature.

The Dutch Wave produced a ripple effect felt across the globe, rekindling interest in native plants, meadow planting, and how plant communities could echo nature in a garden context. It was the basis for so many designers and plant people working today. It's a good point of reference to return to time and again: the idea that it can be radical to simply question why we are doing something. If we have the freedom to question, and the space to think, the idea of the garden will be able to keep evolving, growing away from previously-held beliefs of what it should be.

> "The art of gardening uses living material that has its own laws and prerogatives, which won't allow it to be manipulated by the artist without a struggle. Nevertheless, the history of gardening has witnessed a series of attempts to divest the material of its essence and force it into a straight-jacket."
>
> Henk Gerritsen

THE OUDOLFS' NURSERY OF IDEAS

Piet Oudolf is a living legend among garden designers for his naturalistic style of planting with a focus on perennials and grasses. What many aren't aware of are Oudolf's talent as a plant specialist and nurseryman.

Oudolf's work as a designer includes numerous high-profile commissions, admired around the world. Places like the High Line in New York, the Maximilianpark Hamm in Germany, and Trentham in the U.K. have showcased his aesthetic to millions, and brought naturalistic garden thinking to the mainstream.

But it all started back in the early 1980s, when Hummelo was just a dilapidated farm building and a surrounding few acres of land. Here, on the outskirts of a small village in the rural east of the Netherlands, Oudolf and his wife Anja started their plant nursery. From this humble beginning emerged what would come to be considered the epicenter of a radical gardening movement. The Dutch Wave (or New Perennial movement) saw an exciting shift towards a more natural style of planting, inspired by the way plants grow in their natural habitats. Oudolf's particular planting style calls to mind a prairie meadow, but always held within a garden framework, with a structure of hedges and architectural backbone. People have said that his planting walks the line between freedom and control.

Hummelo, Piet and Anja's private garden, was a test bed for Oudolf's design ideas and planting combinations. It was also a nursery where they grew and trialed many perennial plants. In the early '80s, their nursery hosted a number of open garden days that became the locus of these new ideas. As philosopher and new wave pioneer Rob Leopold said: "The collectively creative spirit was the progressive driving force behind the new movement."

Run primarily by Anja, the nursery at Hummelo built a reputation for its robust and wilder-looking perennials and grasses. It expanded to offer an enormous variety of such plants, which provided Piet with a constant resource for experimenting and evolving his ideas. This benefited not only their private garden, but also his growing raft of commissions. In this sense, the evolution of the Dutch Wave was very much down to Anja's work too—as Piet said on numerous occasions, "without her, all of this wouldn't have been possible."

As the Dutch Wave's philosophy (and the plants associated with it) became more mainstream, the Oudolfs felt they no longer needed to continue with the nursery, and closed in 2010.

Where the nursery had been, a new garden and studio emerged: a perennial meadow, looser and freer than anything in the garden before. The energy and inspiration behind a garden never stops evolving. Hummelo really was a garden that opened many eyes to the endless possibility of taking notes from nature.

OPPOSITE Piet Oudolf, the Dutch master plantsman, stands amidst a sea of perennials at his home—Hummelo. **P.94** An aerial view over the garden, towards the old farmhouse that became the home of Piet and Anja. What were originally fields are now full of verdant naturalistic planting.

ABOVE The many perennial plants offer a rich food source for many pollinators and invertebrates. **OPPOSITE** Seed heads from grasses provide rich texture and movement to the planting.

P. 98 Multiple pathways are a feature of Oudolf's designs; they provide a variety of ways to view and read the garden, encouraging a more three-dimensional, immersive perspective. **P. 100** Hedges and clipped elements create a structural framework for the softer, more fluid plantings of grasses and perennials.

REWILDING AN OVERLOOKED SPACE IN A CASTLE GARDEN

The 3,500-acre (1,416-hectare) Knepp Estate has become synonymous with the concept of rewilding. A farm on low-grade arable soil, the estate returned to natural processes in 2001—and has seen a remarkable transformation since then.

Isabella Tree's *Wilding,* a book documenting this process, brought the project to a much wider audience. But an area of the Knepp estate remained largely untouched by this ethos: the 19th-century walled garden. So the idea came to incorporate some of the lessons learned during the Knepp Wildland project to this particular space.

A collaboration between Tom Stuart-Smith's studio and special advisors Professor James Hitchmough, Jekka McVicar, and Professor Mick Crawley, the team set out to "rewild" this historic garden.

The 1.3-acre (5,260-square-meter) walled garden was previously split into two distinct gardens: one traditional kitchen garden and one monoculture of grass for a croquet lawn and a swimming pool. The cypress and olive trees around the pool are the only thing which remain of the latter, after a profound transformation. The process was initiated by changing the topography of the land—digging out hollows, and creating mounds with the collected soil. This created a dynamism which mirrored similar processes that occur on the estate, where large herbivores constantly shift earth throughout the year. The hollows in the garden flood in wet periods and the mounds create sunny banks, each enriching the garden's potential for biodiversity. This new topography was accompanied by a diversification in soil fertility; achieved in part by adding an 8-inch (20-centimeter) layer of crushed concrete and brick from demolished farm buildings nearby. Mixed with sharp sand, this layer reduced the soil fertility in certain parts of the garden; although this may sound counterintuitive, this allowed the soil to support species that would normally be outcompeted on the Knepp soil. Other areas remained of a higher fertility grade. This provided the garden with the potential for increased diversity not only in terms of plants (of which there are now around 800 species), but also in terms of the insects and animals that live off them.

On the other side, the kitchen garden has seen a more subtle change. It is still a productive space: its no-dig beds still produce a wide variety of edible plants. The lawn and crushed stone paths have become "dirty" paths—meaning a layer of soil and stone has been scattered over them. This provides an environment for herbs and self-seeders to thrive.

Planting began in 2020 and was completed in 2022. This horticultural experiment will be monitored over the coming years; surveys of flora and fauna will be conducted and compared to the baseline, pre-renovation. The gardeners at Knepp will play a key role in observing and evolving this garden as it grows.

ABOVE The kitchen garden—the blurring of "dirty paths" with Mediterranean herbs running into the vegetable beds. **OPPOSITE** In the new half of the garden, plants are left to self-seed; the ivy remains shaggy, providing more habitat options.

P.104 One of the scrapes created in the new garden fills with water during wet periods, creating added biodiversity benefits.

ABOVE The yew tree in the background is clipped to mimic random herbivore grazing. **OPPOSITE** The kitchen garden has a mixture of fruit trees, herbs, and vegetables growing in a mosaic fashion. **P.108** A section of the planting in the new garden that was only completed in 2022—how it evolves will be watched with great interest.

WHAT IS THE FUTURE OF THE GARDEN?

The future of the garden is loaded with potential, and open to our imagination. Perhaps we will approach the garden as more of a shared space, and less of an anthropocentric one.

Much has been written on the environment in the last few years. This ground swell of thinking has sought to put into perspective what has happened, is happening, and how we can move forward in a much more sustainable way. Of course, gardening plays a crucial role in this narrative. Gardens are many people's most tangible point of contact with nature—from their own private gardens, to the public parks and spaces we interact with on a daily basis. The Covid-19 pandemic brought into sharp focus just how important these interactions are, and the positive impact they can have on our lives.

Such works like Emma Marris's *Rambunctious Garden: Saving Nature in a Post-Wild World* and Gilles Clément's *"The Planetary Garden" and Other Writings* make the case for thinking of the world itself as a garden. Clément in particular contemplates how each of us has a personal responsibility as a gardener of the planet. This duty impacts the way we live, and the care we take with our choices. Clément encourages us to live in harmony with the planet, balancing what the earth offers with what we take in a sustainable manner. If you depend on your garden to sustain you, you would not set out to destroy it.

This point brings us back to the idea of ownership. We saw in an earlier chapter that the word "garden" itself is rooted in the notion of enclosure. There's something that feels quite isolationist about the garden's foundation as a space defined by boundaries. It places the focus on what's inside the space, in some sense separating it from nature and what exists beyond the boundary marker. Particularly in the 19th and 20th centuries, the rise of the private suburban garden brought the idea of enclosure even more into focus. Gardening came to signify a collection of disjointed pieces of land, conceptually isolated from the natural world.

But what if we were to think about our gardens from another perspective? What if we considered them as conceptually open spaces? Insects, birds, and other creatures move through, above, and under these spaces. Could we consider our gardens as conduits for nature, and become conscious of the importance of these spaces beyond our own needs?

We have often bought into the idea that biodiversity and nature can survive in a number of fenced-off, protected areas that we classify as "natural." These spaces form islands of refuge in an otherwise sterile and decimated landscape, which we have developed, farmed, sprayed, mined, dammed, and engineered for profit. This idea is rapidly becoming out of date in the context of our current planetary situation. As Marris argues, we

The High Line in New York—the poster child of postindustrial planting.

Moerenuma Park in Sapporo repurposed land that had previously been a landfill.

are entering a post-wild world, and the way we relate to the natural world fundamentally has to change. Our towns and cities must become wilder; they must seek to connect with wilder spaces beyond. The gardens of the future must join up, not enclose.

AN EVOLUTION IN GARDEN THINKING

In postindustrial landscapes across the world, we have borne witness to an ebullient event: nature returning to places that we had previously decimated. One pioneering example is the Landschaftspark Duisburg-Nord in North Rhine-Westphalia, Germany, which opened in 1994 on the vast former Thyssen ironworks. The park—which retains much of the abandoned industrial architecture—can neither be described as entirely natural nor entirely synthetic. Instead, it is a meeting of the two. The park highlights nature's ability to unpick our most formidable industrial visions. This approach is now a globally recognised evolution of the garden and landscape narrative. It has inspired numerous projects around the world, including Park am Gleisdreieck in Berlin, MFO Park in Zurich, and—the poster child of postindustrial gardens—the High Line in New York.

Welcoming nature into urban environments can make our towns and cities more resilient in the face of climate change. The simplicity of the shade offered by trees is a great example that needs no explaining, and something we have all sought out. Beyond this, we can also use nature's processes to help manage other aspects of urban infrastructure. Sustainable Drainage Systems (or SuDS, as they are often referred to) slow and filter rainwater—examples include rain gardens, which are now appearing in numerous cities. They aim to hold on to sudden rain events or cloudbursts, preventing the overflow of sewers and allowing polluted water to enter our rivers and seas. What we must come to terms with is that nature generally has the answers; we must be humble enough to accept our role as collaborator.

It may seem strange to be talking about urban infrastructure and postindustrial projects. How do these reflect back on our own personal gardens? "Wild" gardens have frequently been in focus over the last 40 years. We've seen more native planting, inspired by plant formations found in nature; the prairie garden has been at the front of this wave. But as Clément so rightly points out, these gardens still very much have the garden designer as their author. They are more inspired by nature, perhaps, and there is more cooperation, but rarely are they allowed to evolve of their own free will. Yet these "wasteland" spaces offer hope and inspiration in how to evolve the garden. If we can see a meadow in the uncut grass of a roadside, and acknowledge cycles of decay and rebirth—if we can stop wishing to tidy up nature—we can start to see the garden in a new light. Could we even begin to come to terms with nature having a more active role? Could we begin to see a garden without boundaries? Could we acknowledge gardens as our own personal spaces to engage with, but more importantly as places to nourish ourselves, our imaginations, and our relationships with other living things that surround us? Can we see the garden as being in harmony with nature, as both a teacher, and a bridge?

"Perhaps the gardener is not someone who makes forms survive over time, but over time, ensures that enchantment survives. We must try." Gilles Clément

A POSTWAR VISION FOR A BETTER WORLD

For a celebration of armistice and tranquility, Isamu Noguchi's Garden of Peace certainly attracted controversy. However, Noguchi's interpretation of ancient aesthetics has certainly stood the test of time.

In the aftermath of World War II, the United Nations was established as a forum to transcend national boundaries. It aimed to develop friendly relations among nations, achieve international cooperation, and act as a center for harmonizing the actions of nations. The UN includes a number of specialist agencies, including UNESCO, its Educational, Scientific, and Cultural Organization.

Headquartered in Paris, the UNESCO buildings were inaugurated in 1958, following a collaborative design by three renowned architects from three different countries. As part of the plan for the surrounding landscape, a peace garden was commissioned. The Japanese-American sculptor Isamu Noguchi was chosen to create a space that would offer a place for quiet contemplation, and also speak to the future.

Often referred to as "the Japanese garden," Noguchi's design for the Garden of Peace undoubtedly draws on his Japanese heritage. The garden clearly references Japanese Zen garden design; indeed, Noguchi was assisted by Toemon Sano, a highly regarded Japanese garden master. The arrangement of a number of stones gifted from Japan also forms a key element of the garden. In spite of the clear links to Japanese horticultural history, the garden drew controversy, as some people felt it did not represent a "proper" Japanese garden. UNESCO eventually stepped in, acknowledging that it differs from a traditional Japanese garden, in that it can be viewed as a whole by visitors, uses nontraditional materials such as asphalt, and its maintenance does not allow for traditional rituals to take place on a daily basis. But this reading of the garden perhaps missed the point of commissioning someone like Noguchi. His influences and personal story crossed heritages; his work drew on an ancient outlook for inspiration, but was equally forward-looking in his use of materials. Furthermore, commissioning a sculptor (rather than a landscape designer) for this project speaks to the idea of embracing cultural cross-pollination—an idea that is very much at the heart of UNESCO.

In his own words, Noguchi said: "In Japan the worship of stones changed into an appreciation of nature. The search for the essence of sculpture seems to carry me to the same end."

It somehow seems appropriate that a peace garden for a postwar institution should be the genesis for such heated conversations. But ultimately, the garden has transcended this discourse. It is now rightfully celebrated as a calm and peaceful place in the heart of Paris—one which has the ability to transport us beyond the commotion of the modern world.

OPPOSITE Noguchi's design took into account the fact that many people would be viewing the garden from above, due to the number of tall buildings that surround the site. This was something unfamiliar to a traditional Japanese Zen garden. The strong lines and bold shapes provide a clear framework that reads well from overhead.

P.122 The garden uses a mixture of traditional and contemporary material elements. A number of stones gifted from Japan were placed within the space; equally, asphalt was used too—a contemporary material not found in any traditional Japanese garden. A hybrid approach befitting the institution, perhaps.

A REIMAGINED RIAD GARDEN IN MARRAKESH

When Tom Stuart-Smith's studio was commissioned to redesign the gardens at Jardin Secret in Marrakesh, they knew they would be working with layers of history and culture. Embracing this context added new dimensions to the garden.

In the 19th century, the Jardin Secret was one of the largest riads (a courtyard, or interior garden) in the old city of Marrakesh. In the 16th century, it was the site of the palace of the Saadian Sultan; later, it belonged to the chamberlain of Sultan Moulay Abd al-Hafid, who was the last sultan of Morocco before French rule.

The garden revival began with uncovering the physical layers of this history. The elaborate water system was discovered, which enabled a greater understanding of how water was irrigated to the garden. As the lifeblood of the garden, the water's route could be traced back to the Atlas mountains via the great water basin on the edge of the city. The remains of the 16th-century garden of the Saadian Dynasty were also uncovered. This was a key point in the future plan for the garden: it established that there had been a division between two gardens, as well as a building on the site. These features returned in Stuart-Smith's designs—a pavilion now sits between two courtyards within the riad.

On one side of the pavilion, Stuart-Smith and his team created an Islamic paradise garden, laid out on geometric lines and imposing an order on wild nature. The team were aware of the cultural significance of such a garden; an Islamic garden has profound religious connotations. As this space could be read quite differently to other gardens, there was a major challenge in understanding the cultural context of what this garden represented. Working within and respecting this context gives another layer of complexity to the project.

On the other side, the smaller courtyard of the two features another version of a paradise garden. Inspiration was drawn from the Old Testament's book of Genesis: "out of the ground the Lord God caused to grow every tree that is pleasing to the sight and good for food." Thus, this courtyard houses a wide variety of fruit trees, flowers, and cacti, providing the impression of a lush, exotic space. Opened to the public in 2016, the garden now provides a wonderful and culturally valuable addition to the city.

OPPOSITE A new pavilion now separates the two courtyard gardens within the riad. It was discovered during site excavations that there had been a building historically on this spot, so it seemed fitting in the new scheme Tom Stuart-Smith devised. **P.124** The Islamic garden in the larger of the two courtyards is divided in a traditionally geometric approach; the planting, however, much softer.

ABOVE AND OPPOSITE The second smaller courtyard is inspired by The Old Testament's book of Genesis—"out of the ground the Lord God caused to grow every tree that is pleasing to the sight and good for food." It includes a mixture of fruit trees, herbs, cacti, and flowers, mixed in a naturalistic style.

ABOVE AND OPPOSITE Tones and shapes within the architectural detailing are reflected in the palette of planting for a cohesive and soothing space—ideal for contemplating the world.

REPAIRING AND REDEFINING NATURE'S RESILIENCE

It took almost eight years for Indian landscape legend Prabhakar Bhagwat and his studio to restore the landscape at the Timba basalt quarry, and turn it into a flourishing, self-sustaining ecosystem.

Professor Bhagwat is regarded as a pioneer of landscape architecture in India. Growing up in the Empress Botanical Garden in Pune, where his father was superintendent, set Bhagwat on a path of inspiration and collaboration with the natural world. His son, Aniket Bhagwat, and granddaughter, Vaidehi Bhagwat, continue the legacy by representing the successive generations of the family to become involved at the Prabhakar Bhagwat studio.

With close to 3,000 mines and quarries in India, the country's natural resources are being extracted to feed a global appetite that constantly consumes. The Gujarat region (where the Timba quarry is located) produces a range of minerals, from limestone and silica sand to bauxite and lignite. When the extraction of basalt at the Timba quarry was completed, a scar in the landscape of several hundred acres was left in its wake.

The rejuvenation of the site has been a long process—one based on in-depth knowledge, time, and faith in nature's inherent capacity to heal. The operation involved improving the quality of the soil, which would in turn give a variety of local grasses and trees the foothold needed to regain control. Topsoil was layered on the rock, catalyzing the speed of possible regeneration. A nearby stream was diverted to fill the quarry basin, bringing another dynamic to the scene. The water was populated with fish, which jump-started another local ecosystem. This intense level of intervention meant that the efforts to reintroduce biodiversity and ecological activity at the site rapidly saw success.

The outcome has been to help create and encourage a self-sustaining ecosystem, turning on its head the more familiar hierarchy between humans and nature. By working alongside nature's organic processes, what was once barren at the hands of human intervention is now a thriving forest. This former quarry site at Timba calls into question the ways in which we interact with and use our environment, and also brings to our attention the remarkable resilience of nature, and its ability to heal.

ABOVE The scar left from the basalt quarry, before the project to restore the site began. With close to 3,000 mines and quarries working in India, extracting commodities for a global appetite, this is a vision repeated many times across the country. **OPPOSITE** After eight years, the rejuvenation has resulted in a return of life and a functioning ecosystem.

ABOVE Trees and other native flora found their way back once the soil was improved—layers of fresh topsoil catalyzed the process.

OPPOSITE TOP A nearby stream was diverted, filling the former quarry basin and creating a lake which was populated with fish—in turn jump-starting the creation of another ecosystem within the site.
OPPOSITE BOTTOM The former quarry is now a place where people can go to interact with nature and experience its processes in a living state.

RETHINKING & REGENERATING A SCOTTISH ESTATE

Once home to a baronet's arboretum and 60-acre (24-hectare) rhododendron garden, Corrour Estate has since been reimagined as a self-sustaining haven—while still remaining true to the legacy of the landscape.

Corrour Estate was once the home of Sir John Stirling-Maxwell, a Victorian baronet passionate about botany and forestry. He planted something of an arboretum around the banks of Loch Ossian in Scotland, and also created a rhododendron garden to house the results of various plant-hunting trips to the Himalayas. Its Victorian lodge was lost in a fire in 1943, and the estate came into the care of its current owners in 1995. They had a vision to start a new chapter in Corrour's history.

Architect Moshe Safdie conceived a new lodge made of glass, granite, and steel—something of a contemporary interpretation, in the tradition of Scottish lodges. As this building was beginning to emerge, garden designer Jinny Blom was asked to help connect the building to its context, and to reimagine the surrounding grounds in a more natural fashion.

For Blom, this project provided a chance to work alongside ecologists, foresters, and gamekeepers—not to mention the somewhat degraded but still-inspiring grounds. The client was keen that the garden should largely be self-sustaining, without the need for gardeners. In many ways, this was a project to return the garden to nature. Elements of the Victorian garden still remained, and these were knitted back in around the new building and then out into the wider landscape. In a sense, Blom was creating an "antigarden": one where the boundaries of the garden seem indistinct from the landscape.

Equally, Blom's task extended beyond the remit of a traditional garden. The idea was to turn the 68,000-acre (27,519-hectare) estate into a conservation project. This involved the need for a significant rebalancing of deer numbers, to reduce overgrazing. The erection of an 11-mile (18-kilometer) fenced exclosure provided a chance for natural regeneration of vegetation. The team also tended to and restructured the remaining native and plantation forestry, and restored Sir John Stirling-Maxwell's outstanding legacy of trees around the loch. Sir John had been a founding member of The National Trust for Scotland and Chairman of the Forestry Commission from 1929–32, and his love of trees is clearly apparent. His own approach to the landscape was progressive for his time—and the current owners have brought his ethos into the 21st century.

At Corrour, there is a sense of landscape and garden becoming one—and a sense of healing. The regeneration efforts, and the idea of connection between the lodge and garden, offer a feeling of fluidity and ease that isn't engineered, and has developed organically over time.

ABOVE The new lodge designed by architect Moshe Safdie uses glass, steel, and granite in a modern interpretation of a traditional Scottish lodge. It replaces the previous Victorian incarnation that burned down in 1943. OPPOSITE The degraded landscape of much of the estate will hopefully begin to regenerate once deer numbers are reduced.

P.140 The landscape runs right up to the windows. P.145 The turf roofed sauna on the edge of Loch Ossian—ready to provide a refreshing steam.

A VISION FOR A THOUSAND YEARS

Tokachi Millennium Forest was the brainchild of Mitsushige Hayashi. His vision was to echo the natural environment of Hokkaido, and to promote greater connection between a now largely urban population and the natural world.

Hayashi is the owner of Tokachi Mainichi Newspaper Inc., a national Japanese newspaper business. For this project, he enlisted the help of landscape designers Dan Pearson and Fumiaki Takano. A number of gardens within the project were created to act specifically as visitor attractions, drawing people into different landscape and garden contexts.

Within the garden, a family restaurant looks out onto a series of sculptural raised earth mounds, which echo the mountains in the distance. From inside, they offer a glimpse of the landscape beyond; from outside, they act as something to engage and play with. They call to mind Noguchi's work at Moerenuma Park, and facilitate play and engagement in a similar way.

The Meadow Garden offers naturalistic drifts of perennial planting, including many Japanese natives. Planted in 2008, the Millenium Forest has been a learning process for Pearson, and head gardener Midori Shintani. Over the years, they have seen certain areas of planting succeed, and others diminish. They have sought to find a balance of competition within the plantings; as in nature, certain years will see certain species perform better due to climatic preferences. The garden is always in flux.

Gardening that mimics the natural environment has traditionally been celebrated in Japan, with its long history of a deep reverence and respect for nature. In a 2020 feature for *Garden's Illustrated,* Shintani says:

> We are trying to evoke people's physical sensations and emotions experienced in nature by the naturalistic planting of the Meadow Garden. As we walk along the narrow path like an animal track, the red flowers of *Sanguisorba officinalis* will pop out and touch our shoulders and arms cheerfully. When we walk under the overwhelming height of *Cephalaria gigantea,* our hearts will pound with excitement. Every time we meet a plant, our minds keep moving with feelings of surprise, joy and sometimes fear. Eventually it delivers deep peace to the mind as a memory of 'the nature of the garden,' and we realize that we are a part of nature.

It is this sentiment that Hayashi hoped to engage with in his visionary project at the Tokachi Millennium Forest. If we are to survive as a species, it is intrinsically important that we embrace this idea that we are a part of nature.

ABOVE Raised earth mounds add a sculptural element, echoing the mountains in the distance helping to anchor the garden in its context. OPPOSITE, PP. 146 AND 148 The Meadow Garden, with naturalistic drifts of perennial planting that includes many Japanese natives. PP. 154 AND 155 Woodland planting drifts through the trees in the Millenium Forest with a light and ethereal quality.

AN EXPERIMENT IN COEXISTING IN MEXICO

Natural cycles and connection to place are the foundations of this project by Robert Hutchison Architecture and JSa Arquitectura, which sits in the mountains to the west of Mexico City.

Rain Harvest Home integrates with the landscape to offer its inhabitants an experimental connection to place. The design separates the traditional notion of a house into three structures scattered around the landscape. Each of these spaces provides covered outdoor space, further merging the structures with the terrain. The goal was to create buildings which disturbed the natural landscape as little as possible—to accept nature as a stage, where architecture merely plays a role.

Located near the town of Temascaltepec, (whose name derives from the pre-Hispanic *temazcal,* referring to bathhouses and sweat lodges), Rain Harvest Home works regeneratively with water. Its trio of buildings each collect rainwater, connecting to a reservoir for onsite treatment and storage that supplies 100 percent of the home's water year-round. During extreme wet seasons, excess rainwater is fed back into the neighborhood's water system.

The site also aims to work regeneratively with the soil. It contains a bioagricultural garden and orchard, where fruit and vegetables are grown. As well as its obvious benefit as a food source, these productive elements also help to improve the soil quality, which has become depleted over time. The independent nature of each part of the home encourages further interaction between the landscape and garden: as you move between the main living space, the studio, and the bathhouse, you cannot help but reimmerse yourself in the landscape. The paths that connect the buildings double as bioswales, guiding rainwater to the home's reservoirs and preventing erosion.

The physical and metaphorical center of the home is the circular, open-air bathhouse. This includes a hot bath, sauna, steam shower, and washroom, encircling a central cold plunge pool open to the sky. A place to ritualistically experience the healing qualities of water, the bathhouse serves as a microcosm for the project's larger self-contained water system—a functional monument to this life-giving resource. Rain Harvest Home expands the definition of "personal place" by serving as a platform not just for familial comfort, but also as a laboratory for learning how to coexist with the earth's natural systems. Understanding that the home's water and food systems are part of a living process that fluctuates depending on natural conditions, the inhabitants treat the home as an ongoing experiment, constantly testing new ways to optimize the system through seasonal calibrations. In the process, they become closer to the rhythm of the Earth, and the positive relationships that fosters.

OPPOSITE The living roof of the main house helps it sit more comfortably in its surroundings. **P.156** Paths that connect the buildings also act as bioswales, guiding rainwater to the homes' reservoirs. **P.158** The garden and landscape appear as if without boundaries.

ABOVE The open-air bathhouse includes a hot bath, sauna, steam shower, and washroom encircling a central cold-plunge pool open to the sky. **OPPOSITE** Each building provides covered outside space, which further blends inside and outdoor life.

REVEALING THE SPIRIT OF PLACE

An abandoned quarry and surrounding hillside in the Hudson Valley, Manitoga is the former home of designers Mary & Russel Wright. It is a celebration of the rocks, water, and Northeastern deciduous forest of the United States.

Mary Small Einstein Wright and her husband and business partner Russel Wright were successful industrial designers who believed that good home design could improve people's lives. In 1942, they purchased a ravaged quarry in the Hudson Valley as a weekend retreat outside of New York City. The estate lies on the unceded land of the Wappinger people; Wright named it after the Algonquin word for "Place of Great Spirit."

Sadly, Mary died of breast cancer in 1952, a year after adopting their baby daughter Annie. For years, Russel explored the land with his daughter, and together they observed the vegetation: the lush moss underfoot, majestic oaks, tulips, and white pine trees. The steep ravines and stream crossed a woodland full of species of ferns and wildflowers with dramatic views over the valley. It was this sense of observation that would guide and inform the garden's evolution.

In 1955, Russel was asked by the State Department to tour Southeast Asia to help U.S. exports, and during this trip he fell for Japanese design. By 1957, he was working with architect David L. Leavitt (who had worked with Frank Lloyd Wright in Japan) to build a house at Manitoga. Dragon Rock, as the house became known (a name given by the young Annie Wright), notably sits in the rock cliff, not on it.

Beyond the house, the garden emerged. This was not a man-made design instantly imposed on the landscape; rather, it was a process. Firstly, the observations over years provided an intimacy and connection to place. Secondly, recognition of significant forms, relationships, and patterns within the landscape influenced the development. Thirdly, the dramatization of these elements made them clear to the casual visitor less attuned to the land. Equally important was the way in which movement was guided by Wright to shift the visitor from passive observer to having a more active role in engaging with place. The design poses Manitoga as an interconnected whole, with the visitor guided through careful transitions from place to place.

Like the Japanese stroll garden:

> One is carried through this experience as though the course of footpaths had a musical rhythm. From the shadows of the thicket, one suddenly emerges upon a spacious view... One 'creates' the garden by walking through it. The blueprint is there, and a most winning one it is too, but the experience is created by the viewer.

In this sense Wright, working with the land, found a place of great spirit that shines through for all to see.

ABOVE From inside the house, you are constantly reminded of the closeness to nature—with rocks and vegetation seemingly part of the construction. **OPPOSITE BOTTOM** The remains of the old quarry face can still be seen.

P.164 Paths spread out from the house following routes through the surrounding forest; they reference the Japanese stroll garden in their exploration and engagement with the landscape. **P.166** A small stream was diverted to create the quarry pond. **P.168** The house, built into, not onto, the rock sits within the landscape.

A SLOW DISCOVERY OF BEAUTY

Tokyo's Nezu Museum boasts an outstanding collection of classical Japanese arts. Beyond the museum, set alongside a building designed by Kengo Kuma on the site of Nezu's former home, flows a garden offering a journey of discovery.

The Nezu Museum garden takes the form of a Japanese stroll garden. The idea is to take the observer on a journey—walking along a carefully constructed path with a succession of thoughtfully choreographed points of interest, creating a place for contemplation.

The Japanese stroll garden is perhaps the easiest type of Japanese garden to read from a Western perspective. Culturally, the garden conjures very different associations in Japan. Here, nature is placed at the center of everything—an approach that has been much more slowly adopted in Western gardening traditions. Scenes are spread throughout the stroll garden, hidden from each other yet anticipated; they often call to mind well-known areas of natural beauty. These tableaux do not seek to mimic the areas that inspired them, but do evoke a sense of awe and wonderment at the beauty of nature.

Railway magnate Nezu Kaichirō purchased the land in 1906. He was particularly drawn to its topography; the movement of peaks and valleys gave the potential for added interest in the creation of the garden. Thus the garden was originally conceived in the *shin-zan-yūkoku* style, which conjured the atmosphere of deep mountains and mysterious valleys. The finished design includes teahouses, rustic buildings, pools, stone sculptures, and a small shrine.

Nezu was in fact a passionate practitioner of The Way of Tea (the ceremonial preparation of tea); four teahouses are found at points along the garden path. Inside, the host can offer his guests the intimacy of the tea ceremony, where a world of focused appreciation is shared and observed. The beauty of the surrounding gardens adds a heightened sense of transcendence.

After Nezu's death, the house and collection were opened to the public in 1941. Sadly, the site was largely destroyed during the bombing of Tokyo—but luckily, the museum collection had already been removed. Since then, little by little, the museum and its garden have been restored.

This garden now provides a special oasis in the heart of bustling Tokyo, offering visitors to the museum a chance to escape. The garden still manages to create those timeless moments of intimacy that only nature can provide.

ABOVE One of a number of teahouses found throughout the garden. Inside, the host can offer their guests the tea ceremony, with the beauty of the surroundings adding to the sense of transcendence.

P. 176 In Japan, the approach to the garden is very different from in the West. Here, nature is placed at the center, and a sense of awe and wonder are evoked. Seasons are celebrated, and here the Japanese maples herald the arrival of fall.

ABOVE A *tōrō*, or Japanese stone lantern. **OPPOSITE** Stone sculptures, rustic buildings, and a small shrine are found along the way through the garden. **P.178** Nezu Museum garden takes the form of a Japanese stroll garden—the idea of which is to take the observer on a journey, walking along a carefully constructed path—along which are a series of carefully choreographed points of interest.

ABOVE Natural processes at work in the garden. In the Japanese approach, details and nature are both observed and celebrated. **OPPOSITE** Another teahouse found along the path through the Nezu Museum garden.

WHAT IS A GARDEN?

Perhaps it is easier to start with what a garden isn't: a garden is not static. Through many different styles and epochs, we are still learning what a garden is, and could be.

When we are looking through beautiful images of gardens, it is easy to forget that we are not looking at fixed works of art. What we're seeing are creations that mix the work of humans with the constantly shifting, always evolving forces of nature.

In terms of etymology, the word garden is derived from the Old High German *gard* or *gart,* meaning an enclosure, evolving into French and Middle English as *jardin* and *gardin* respectively, before arriving at the present-day English. These words are formulated around the idea of enclosure, of confinement: a piece of the land within the wider landscape. Throughout history, the garden has been many things: an area that could be physically managed; a space that could produce a crop and help nourish a community; a place for contemplation and prayer; a sanctuary from the wilderness beyond its boundaries.

Within these boundaries large and small, ideas began to flourish about what this space was—and, eventually, could be. In Western traditions, the garden became a manifestation of how humans saw their place in society and the world. More and more, they captured our anthropocentric view, which saw the garden evolve into a theater, and a display of wealth, power, and politics.

Until the Italian Renaissance, beginning in the 15th century, the medieval garden in Italy had been a place for growing herbs and vegetables, and also, in the case of many monastic gardens, a place for prayer and meditation. With the arrival of the great cultural shift of the Renaissance, the garden was elevated to the status of a work of art, swelling in scale and in ambition. Inspired by the gardening ideals of ancient Rome, Renaissance gardens were playful, entertaining, and filled with ideas. In a way, they created a parallel universe, where nature was controlled and orderly—a vehicle for human endeavor and fantasy.

This approach circulated around Europe, evolving as it spread. The most well-known of its incarnations is the French formal garden, or *jardin à la française*. As a garden style, it is the epitome of control, purposefully representing the concept of order in nature. As with other Renaissance styles, the French formal garden heavily incorporated symmetry, geometry, and perspective: trees and plants were clipped and regimented, forming a language more familiar to architecture or sculpture than the natural world. The apogee of this formula is André Le Nôtre's Gardens of Versailles. Commissioned by Louis XIV in 1661, the Gardens of Versailles were the largest garden in Europe at the

OPPOSITE Gravetye Manor, the home and garden of William Robinson. Robinson was a pioneer in imagining the garden in a different, "wilder" way—a radical notion in the 19th century.

time, spanning some 37,066 acres (15,000 hectares). In honor of the "Sun King," the gardens were laid out on an east-west axis, following the sun's journey. It was an enormous garden with exquisite views—but equally encompassed a multitude of smaller enclosures, choreographing spaces for pleasure and intrigue.

By the early 18th century, a new approach was beginning to emerge—one that was seemingly the antithesis of the French style. The English landscape garden started to use a different language to that of architecture, instead seeking out an idealized version of nature. The most familiar name of this epoch is Lancelot "Capability" Brown. He allegedly earned his nickname by telling his clients he could see great "capability" in their unperfected landscapes. Creating lakes that evoked rivers and moving vast amounts of earth to better frame a composition of the landscape—Brown likened himself to a poet or composer, but he was certainly also an engineer. Brown oversaw 170 gardens and landscapes for the upper echelons of British society in his lifetime. For his clients, lavish gardens were part of a wider narrative of fashion and wealth. In many ways, Brown's work reads no differently than the French formal style, differing only in visual language. Fundamentally, the English garden was a perfected pastoral scene, in which nature was compliant; the French garden was a perfected architectural composition, where nature was also compliant.

Of course, throughout all of this, the humble peasant and cottage gardens remained largely unchanged. They were still places where crops were grown, families were nourished, and personal interactions with the earth took place. It wasn't until the late 19th century—with the arrival of a burgeoning middle class, increasing urbanization, and rising aspirations—that the garden became a middle-class leisure interest for many.

In this period, at the height of European colonialism, the garden's potential once again shifted. Vast numbers of species were transported and transplanted across the globe, opening people's imagination to botanical worlds they could never have dreamed of. Scientific advancements influenced the ways people were thinking about nature—but during this time, there was also a growing awareness of, and conflict with, human industrialization. These developments were creating unprecedented changes in the landscape. Naturalists like John Muir spoke out about the importance of wilderness, and giving value to the space beyond the enclosure. Gardener and writer William Robinson coined the term "wild garden" for the title of his hugely influential book, one of a number he wrote about a more natural approach to gardening for a wide middle-class readership. But those same middle classes were buying and building new homes—and for many of them, the garden represented status. The accumulation of tangible assets as a statement of success had arrived. It was a concept that mushroomed throughout the 20th century—the explosion of suburban constructs around the world created spider webs of enclosures around towns and cities. Quite removed from the wider landscape, they became a symbol of nature distilled into its simplest form: a patch of grass, subjugated with chemicals and power tools. The garden space had come to be defined in terms of real estate.

Of course, this is an oversimplification; throughout all of this, the garden remained a font of imagination and

Within these boundaries large and small, ideas began to flourish about what this space was—and, indeed, could be.

One of the many "natural rooms" within Versailles' landscape design, where planting is reduced to pattern making and geometry.

inspiration, and a place to worship in nature's temple. Just as one avenue pursued a course of reduction with regards to the natural world, another has sought a wilder, gentler touch, holistically reconnecting the garden to the bigger picture.

So, this is a boiled-down version of our cultural journey with the garden through modern Europe, from simple enclosures of green spaces, to the garden space as a work of art. We have played with nature, dominated nature, and improved nature. But one question this brief history of the garden does not answer is: what is a garden on the human level? How can we define that feeling of what a garden is? The garden is a sensory and emotional experience—one that often rewards glacially slow observation and contemplation. It is a muse to artists and writers, fuelling countless creative energies. It is a sanctuary in its most literal sense, often providing safe spaces for queer stories and anti-war statements, if we think of places like Sissinghurt or Dixter, all in southeast England.

Beyond the narrative of modern history, if we strip away the fashions and aesthetics of different epochs, what are we left with? A garden is a space, a garden is potential; it is always changing and evolving. A garden is an interaction.

A garden is a meeting point, where human hands touch the earth—and the Earth. At its most poetic, it is an endless dance of nature and the imagination. It can be many things to many people, and the answer to this question is not fixed. Our perceptions of the garden and experiences of it are ever changing.

A garden is never static.

BIO ARCHITECTURE: AN ORGANIC SERPENT IN THE TREES

El Nido de Quetzalcóatl (or Quetzalcóatl's Nest) is the creation of architect Javier Senosiain, one of the first organic architects in Mexico. Organic architecture was a term first coined by Frank Lloyd Wright, with the idea of integrating the built environment into nature, or vice versa.

Senosiain's work often evokes elements of the natural world: shells, animals, and waterfalls. In the case of El Nido de Quetzalcóatl, the main inspiration was a snake. The serpentine building houses 10 apartments, which wind their way around the rugged topography of the site. El Nido de Quetzalcóatl not only takes its inspiration from nature, but also seeks to create as little negative environmental impact from its presence as possible.

It connects to Senosiain's vision of "Bio-Architecture," which places the focus on using materials and techniques that provide the best results in terms of energy and resource consumption. It also aims to reduce the amount of pollution generated during construction, and even during the production of the construction materials. The ecological impact of every phase of development is considered.

El Nido de Quetzalcóatl is named after the feathered serpent from ancient Mexican lore. Snaking its way through caves, ravines, and an oak forest, Senosiain's work took what most would have seen as obstacles and turned them into inspiration. It's an architecture that rejects geometric lines, and is infused with natural and ecological thinking. The contours of the landscape guided the shape of the building, allowing this serpent to emerge naturally from the design. The main structure is made of ferro-cement (where lime or plaster is poured over a supporting metal structure); multicolored and iridescent, it was designed to resemble the feathers of the Quetzalcóatl. In addition to the apartments, this structure also houses several stained-glass domes which rain down color onto their interiors, and "The Egg": a windowless, round, entirely white space with a giant circular couch, perfect for meditation and contemplation. It culminates in a giant serpent's head on the roof, whose open jaw offers beautiful views of the landscape.

Around the apartments lies a 1.2-acre (0.5 hectare) park with various gardens for cacti, herbs, and vegetables. There are also greenhouses, and a grass-covered amphitheater. An array of ponds and waterfalls bring another energy to the garden, as do the many walls and serpentine structures covered in mosaic scales.

This magical creation just 15 miles (24 kilometers) from central Mexico City highlights what is possible if we follow paths beyond the familiar, and engage with the kaleidoscope of inspiration offered to us by the natural world.

ABOVE AND OPPOSITE Snaking its way through the site, El Nido de Quetzalcóatl is named after the feathered serpent of ancient Mexican lore. It is manifested in modern materials of ferro-cement and thousands of mosaic pieces, giving it an iridescent and multicolored presence in the landscape.

OPPOSITE, PP. 200 AND 201 The serpentine building houses 10 apartments; the shapes within the building continue in an organic fashion, with curving walls and irregular windows. In addition to the apartments, the structure also houses several stained-glass domes, which function as greenhouses and rain color down onto the plants.

A RADICAL PLOT THAT KEEPS INSPIRING NEW DIRECTIONS

When Richard Christiansen bought the run-down Flamingo Estate in the hills of Los Angeles, he was drawn to its story. Hedonistic and alternative, the roots of Flamingo are still alive and well today.

The pink buildings of Flamingo Estate sit within a verdant 7-acre (3-hectare) garden that hums with pollinators, produce, and the whispers of its past. Parties, music, and mischief filled the air during the estate's earliest incarnation as a radical outpost in 1940's L.A. The estate was created by two men looking to establish their own vision of an earthly paradise. This image of a garden of earthly delights inspired Christiansen as he set about returning the estate to its former glory.

But what started out as a renovation project soon expanded, as the garden provided an epiphany that shifted Christiansen's life focus. The garden had slowly been working its magic on Christiansen, but it was during the pandemic that the full force of its powers became apparent.

Growing up in a farming family, Christiansen had always felt a strong connection to nature, and it was during this enforced period of reflection that it returned. This connection was pulled into sharp focus when a friend's farm was threatened with bankruptcy, due to a loss of produce sales to the shuttered restaurant and hospitality industries. The idea to sell produce from this farm (and several others) from the parking lot of Christiansen's Highland Park bookstore seemed slightly crazy—but it was an instant success. The event grew from week to week, and selling vegetable boxes was leading the way to a new business plan. Flamingo Estate now works with over 75 farms, all of which use regenerative practices or are moving towards them. Flamingo Estate describes their collective of growers as "a bunch of ardent dreamers who are fighting to preserve the natural world—with green thumbs and middle fingers." They place a strong emphasis on healthy living soils, respect for watersheds, and refraining from using pesticides. Their ethcs is all about growing in harmony with nature, rather than robbing her blind. Christiansen's passion for the bounties of mother nature has been reignited in a dramatic way. Being able to see his garden as the birthplace of all that sustains us is the fruit of his labor of love at Flamingo Estate.

OPPOSITE A long flight of stairs descends from the house down into the lushness of the garden. **P. 204** French architects Karl Fournier and Olivier Marty of Studio KO helped Richard realize his dream of a bathhouse on the property. All water is recycled for use in the garden.

PP. 208 AND 213 Some of the exceptional produce from the garden at Flamingo. **P. 209** Honey bees and an apiary on the estate help pollinate and provide honey.

HOUWELING'S
TOMATOES
GREENHOUSE GROWN
TOMATOES
PRODUCT OF USA

HARVEST 16
FLAMINGO
ESTATE

ABOVE AND OPPOSITE The gardens at Flamingo Estate have inspired a whole new business venture, focused on the bounty of mother nature's produce. **PP. 210 AND 211** Works of art punctuate the garden and pathways that meander through the estate.

"GOD, TO ME, IS NATURE"

Robert Burle Marx was one of the most influential landscape architects of the 20th century. He championed native plants, and living in connection with nature—perhaps nowhere more so than on his eponymous site.

Burle Marx's career rapidly took off following his first commission in 1932. He helmed a number of high profile public and private projects, including public parks in Malaysia, and in his native Brazil. By 1942 he was in a position to purchase a 90-acre (36.5-hectare) estate with his brother: the Sítio de Santo Antônio da Bica, now known as Sítio Roberto Burle Marx. The brothers sought out a plot with a good diversity of soil and native vegetation. Located in the west of Rio de Janeiro, the site consisted of mangrove, Atlantic forest, and restinga: a type of coastal tropical and subtropical broadleaf forest found in northeastern Brazil.

Burle Marx frequently spoke of his deep connection to nature, and it was at the Sítio that he really got to expand and explore this relationship. Over the last two decades of Burle Marx's life, the Sítio became a vast laboratory, encompassing gardens, nurseries, and the tropical plant collection he had amassed. 3,500 species of tropical and subtropical plants were organized here, amongst the native vegetation of the site. Burle Marx's house—which he restored and extended over a number of years—could also be found amongst the gardens and vegetation. Also situated here is the studio Burle Marx built in the 1970s. It consists of the façade of a neoclassical townhouse that Burle Marx purchased when it was due to be demolished in central Rio, and a modern structure of concrete and glass which he had built behind it. His studio is a perfect example of the way Burle Marx knitted together many disparate elements into a whole. Other structures are scattered around the site, including libraries, administrative buildings, and the Graziela Maciel Barroso Shade House: a section of nurseries named after the first woman to apply to be a naturalist at the garden in 1946. Barroso became a close friend to Burle Marx, and went on to identify over 100 plant species, as well as teaching Brazilian botanists for over 50 years.

Sítio Roberto Burle Marx evolved to become a truly inspiring synthesis of culture and nature, now covering an area of 100 acres (40.5 hectares) and housing a staggering diversity of plants, art collections, and gardens. It is the legacy of not only Burle Marx, but also of the group of people who sought to actively highlight the incredible diversity of Brazilian flora. This group also performed critical ecological work, speaking out against the destruction of indigenous species through logging, mining, and farming. In 1985, Sítio Roberto Burle Marx became a special unit linked to the National Institute of Historical and Artistic Heritage, recognizing its importance to so many different fields.

ABOVE Sítio Roberto Burle Marx contains a vast collection of 3,500 species of tropical and subtropical plants—growing amongst the native vegetation on the site.

OPPOSITE TOP Burle Marx's studio can be seen, with its neoclassical front that was saved from a demolition in central Rio. Behind this sits a modern structure of concrete and glass that Burle Marx had built—it has been described as the perfect example of how the architect knitted together different elements into a whole.

ABOVE A number of buildings are spread across Sítio Roberto Burle Marx. This is the Santo Antônio da Bica Chapel. It dates from the end of the 18th century, built in colonial style that was restored in the 1970s by architects Lúcio Costa and Carlos Leão.

OPPOSITE The loggia is a modern interpretation of Brazilian and Portuguese cultural traditions, with the blue tile panels designed by Burle Marx in 1967. It looks out onto the gardens through stone-framed arches.

OPPOSITE One of the many lakes and pools that feature throughout the gardens. They vary in style, from natural looking to highly designed creations with elaborate stone detailing and cascades.
ABOVE The lush vegetation is a collage of every color of green under the sun.

ABOVE A display of various bromeliads in a high-rise metal planting structure. **OPPOSITE TOP** Burle Marx's house looking out onto a pond; the house was extended and renovated to its current state over a number of years. Throughout, the colonial elements of the design were preserved: its single-story construction, whitewashed walls, and blue-painted windows and doors.

OPPOSITE BOTTOM The reverse side of the pond wall outside Burle Marx's house—highly sculptural and with plants sprouting from various cracks and crevices.

POINTS OF VIEW

Perceptions can be hard to change—but if we can reconsider what is "messy" and "natural" in a garden, we can begin to undo years of thinking that have separated the garden from the rhythms of nature.

The way we see the world is, to a large extent, inherited. Only by questioning the familiar can we start to see things with fresh eyes.

As we discovered in previous chapters, much of what we understand about the garden is tied up with the narrative of human history, and how we think about the world. For many, the garden remains tangled up with ideas of control, ownership, and status. But there are gardeners who see the garden in looser terms, as something more natural. Such gardeners often use the word "messy" to describe their spaces. We tend to focus on the negative associations of the word messy, picturing a space that has not been cared for, or one that is out of control. But when it comes to messy gardens, it is better to think of messy in terms of synonyms like complex, tangled, and intricate.

Particular elements of the garden are held in the psyche, and visualized a particular way. For example, the lawn: it is easy enough for most of us to picture a lawn, but do we imagine a lawn that is freshly cut, or unkempt? What does this lawn represent in the way it looks?

A colonial export from Europe, the lawn has become a particularly important construct—especially in terms of the American dream. In this way, the lawn might seem to represent the colonization of nature. The rise of monoculture across vast areas of the United States cannot go unacknowledged; this monoculture speaks to homogeneity not just in terms of plant species, but also in terms of society. The perfect green carpet laid out as the plinth for your real estate, the lawn shows the world you have arrived, that you are a success story in the ideology of the American dream. Of course, the roll out of turf is not confined to the U.S.—a well-managed lawn is a symbol of affluence and success across South America, Asia, Australia, and the Middle East.

The trouble is, that dream comes at a huge ecological cost—particularly in those arid places where grass is far from natural. Irrigated, fertilized, treated with herbicide and fungicide: lawns are big business. The volume of resources they consume and the amount of pollution they create is quite staggering—lawns are far removed from a vision of a green future.

However, this is not to say that all lawns are bad! A lawn can offer many benefits in the right climatic context—not in the least as a good place to sit, play, and entertain. The lawn is ultimately meadow: admittedly refined and regulated, but waiting to return to its natural state, given half a chance. In recent years, declining

Weeds are just a construct, a specific way of seeing the garden.

Gilles Clément in his garden—his observations of nature inform his approach.

bee and invertebrate populations have sparked efforts to change people's perceptions of their lawns. Activists have recast the lawn from a green desert with slim pickings for insects, to a space buzzing with life. In the U.K., Plantlife: The Wild Plant Conservation Charity initiated No Mow May, a campaign that, as its name suggests, encourages gardeners to leave their lawns to grow through the month of May. This leaves any flowering species in the sward—such as clovers, dandelions and daisies—to flower, providing an extra boost to pollinators. The charity highlights that since the 1930s, 7.5 million acres of wildflower meadow have been lost in the U.K.—and that Britain's 15 million gardens could, in some way, help offset that enormous decline.

Professor of Biological Sciences Dave Goulson points out in his book *The Garden Jungle* that a meadow doesn't need to be large: a single square meter is a good start, if that's all you can spare. He also discusses the idea of neighborly anxiety in letting lawns grow, suggesting that a mown path can be a good way of making the concept look "planned." If you can't bear to totally let go, Goulson also highlights that there are many benefits to simply mowing less frequently.

In places where lawns are environmentally unsuitable, a different, more climate-appropriate approach has emerged. Xeriscaping, as it's become known, is gardening that reduces or removes the need for additional irrigation. It has proven popular in parts of the western United States and Australia. Some residents in California have even been offered financial incentives to convert their lawns. The city of Novato's water department estimated that residents who had switched to xeriscaping saved 120 gallons (450 liters) of water a day. They also no longer had gardens that looked alien to the landscape, imposing some idealized notion of what a garden should look like, but rather ones that celebrated the climate and locality of where they were. An increase in climate-appropriate native plants is also an added boost to local biodiversity, given that native plants are increasingly being pushed out of their familiar land due to intensive farming and development pressures.

It's not only the lawn where we have unpicked nature's processes and engineered our own to the point of absurdity. Our gardening routines and habits, learned and taught, often involve ideas of perfection. With not a flower out of place or a leaf on the ground, many gardens are expected to be as neat and tidy as a room in the house, and are held to quite unnatural standards. If only we could see things differently—those perennials that we race to cut down at the end of the season could provide shelter for invertebrates and food for birds through the winter. The leaf litter we so hurriedly sweep away and collect could in fact be a layer of nourishment that will return to the soil. There are methods in nature's cycles that make sense, should we choose to observe a little more, and develop a more open-minded perspective.

Taking a more hands-off role in the garden can feel a little alien to many people, who see gardening as an action, something that must be rigorously maintained. But gardening in collaboration with nature in a holistic way offers so much more than a never-ending pursuit of perfection: it's a never-ending journey of enlightenment.

"The question is not what you look at, but what you see."

Henry David Thoreau, *I to Myself*

A RETURN TO NATURE: THE "ANTIGARDEN"

A Tudor half-timbered farmhouse reclaimed by nature, partly hidden under a festoon of climbers, and surrounded by planting that emerges at every opportunity: this was the vision for Jinny Blom's "antigarden."

Blom was asked by her client to help turn this 40-acre (16-hectare) former high-input dairy farm into an idealized vision of a preindustrial landscape. The idea was that the space should benefit human and nonhuman residents alike, and that it should be gardened and designed in a way that prioritizes nature. The term "antigarden" was used to articulate the desire to create a naturalizing garden: one that still holds the form of a classic English garden, but that behaves very differently.

Somewhat appropriately, the design has been overlaid onto the existing hard landscaping; the addition of layers of soft planting that contain many self-seeders creates the fascinating illusion of a garden reclaiming the built environment, and adds an ethereal quality to the whole scene. The previous lawns were transformed into vegetable beds and a series of three meadows, each with a different mix of species.

The planting here is clearly focused on supporting as wide a diversity of species as possible. Habitat and food sources for birds and invertebrates encourage an ecosystem that is bursting with life. This productive element is also carried across in other planting, with a focus on the use of herbs, fruits, vegetables, and medicinal plants throughout. The garden extends out into the wider farm, with a woodland nuttery, an orchard, and fruit-rich hedgerows (some laid, and some left to grow out), providing a diversity of habitats which run naturally into the sweet chestnut coppice that flanks the property. Even a number of dead espalier apple trees feature in the garden. They not only lend the garden a sculptural quality, but also remain productive in a way we do not typically celebrate: by providing a home for a range of invertebrates and fungi that can only exist in such environments.

Poignantly, this wild-looking garden does not simply let nature run its course. A gardener works full-time to ensure this balance between nature and garden is perfectly calibrated and maintained. They also make sure species competition remains mixed, thus creating the widest potential offering in terms of biodiversity. The relationship between gardener and nature can be a tremendously positive one—and as this garden proves, their collaboration can yield enchanting results.

ABOVE Lawns were turned into vegetable beds and three meadows, each with a different plant mix. **OPPOSITE TOP** The house is festooned with climbers, and planting emerges at every opportunity through the preexisting hard landscaping.

P. 234 Even a number of dead espalier apple trees feature in the garden, adding a sculptural element while providing another habitat for fungus and invertebrates that feed or live on dead wood.

A WILD WELSH GARDEN IN THE WOODS

High in the Black Mountains of the Brecon Beacons National Park in Wales lies Nant-y-Bedd: a garden amongst the trees of a thick conifer woodland. The surrounding nature inspires—and is welcomed into—the garden.

For over 40 years, the garden at Nant-y-Bedd has been evolving and growing into the landscape. To be more precise, the landscape and the garden have been growing together. The garden "welcomes the spontaneity of self-seeders and wildflowers." Nant-y-Bedd is very much a natural garden—both in its setting, and in the way it blurs into the woodland that embraces it.

At the heart of the garden sits an ivy-clad, former forester's cottage, the home of Sue and Ian Mabberley. The Mabberleys are passionate about growing organic fruit and vegetables, and the transformative power that comes from growing your own produce. Thus, Nant-y-Bedd is not just a beautiful wild space—it's also a productive one. This is informed by a philosophy of the garden that sees it as a beacon for living in a more sustainable way. The Mabberleys put this philosophy into practice throughout the garden, by planting to enhance the garden's biodiversity and wildlife, producing soil-enriching compost, and generating micro hydropower from the stream that runs through it. The focus is placed on circular and regenerative growing. More than just a garden, Nant-y-Bedd is part of a living landscape—one that sustains and inspires.

Sue began creating the garden 40 years ago—since then, it has expanded in both size and scope. It now stretches over 10 acres (4 hectares), incorporating some of the woodland previously on its borders, and creating an even more direct link to the surroundings. It also now encompasses the stream that gave the garden its name: Nant-y-Bedd is Welsh for "Stream of the Grave." This stream emerges from the top of the mountain, where two Bronze Age burial mounds lie. The garden also includes a natural swimming pond, wildflower meadows, an edible forest garden, a potager, a cottage garden, and plenty of places to pause and admire the harmony of the place.

Nant-y-Bedd speaks to the spirit of the garden as a living part of life, and the ways it can sustain us, both physically and emotionally. Beyond this, the garden is also part of the comprehensive ecosystem that includes us and all who we share the earth with. Ultimately, Nant-y-Bedd is a joyful garden that isn't bound by its boundaries.

ABOVE A rope bridge over the stream leads away from the main garden towards the wildflower meadows and pond beyond. **P. 238** A rainwater collection point set amongst an array of potted plants.

P. 242 A cottage garden surrounds the ivy-clad former forester's cottage, the home of Sue and Ian Mabberley, creators of Nant-y-Bedd. **P. 244** The shepherd's hut, set in the trees next to the natural swimming pond.

TRIAL & OBSERVATION: THE GARDEN AS TEACHER

A disused Victorian walled garden has become a testing ground for gardener James Horner's horticultural practice. Here, Horner watches how chosen varieties grow, interrelate, and thrive.

When given the opportunity to plant in the abandoned walled garden, Horner could see the tremendous potential in the space. With no trace left of the historical garden that had once grown here, it was a landscape in transition. The soil was somewhat rested, and a number of young saplings were beginning to emerge. Five English oaks towards the center (which had emerged during a mast year) gave James a natural starting point for creating the new garden.

Horner was a recent graduate of the traineeship at nearby Great Dixter (p. 16), where he had been schooled in the most fundamental skill of all gardeners: the skill of observation. A gardener's relationship with any garden is a long one, played out over seasons and years. This garden space offered the perfect opportunity to develop such a relationship, and to evolve Horner's practice.

Engaging with the whole 2-acre (8,100-square-meter) plot at once would have been overwhelming, so Horner began by engaging with a single area the size of a tennis court. The soil was heavily compacted, made worse by the heavy Weald clay: reviving the soil health was one of the first major lessons the garden would provide. After two years, things were much improved, and the cultivated area was expanded again to its current size (roughly a quarter of the walled space).

As a trial garden, much of the space is divided by long narrow beds for ease of access, and broad mown paths. Organizing it this way helps keep its purpose and function in focus. Within these beds, plants are observed, their habits and preferences noted. Within this context, successes and failures are both equally important to learning more about the space and plants. "Once I feel I have grasped the key characteristics of a plant and found a method of increasing it, I am then free to be liberal with it," Horner says.

A plant's vigor, climate hardiness, and disease resistance are all considered before its aesthetic qualities. No pesticides or fertilizers are used, and there is no irrigation beyond initial establishment. This way, Horner has a greater understanding of the individual plants, which results in fewer unsuccessful projects in his wider work. This saves effort, time, and waste on his large private commissions. This garden is a privilege that is not lost on Horner, and has only strengthened his relationship to plants and nature. It continues to inspire and school him in equal measure.

ABOVE Gardener and plantsman James Horner with cuttings from his garden. **OPPOSITE** Entrance to the abandoned 19th-century walled garden that James has taken on. **P. 250** As a trial garden much of the space is divided into long narrow beds, with broad mown paths for ease of access.

OPPOSITE TOP One of the English oaks that formed a natural starting point for where to start the garden. The self-seeded saplings from a mast year were one of the signs showing how long the garden had been left alone. **P. 254** Horner surveying a sea of flowers within the walled garden in Sussex.

NATURE'S GENIUS: OBSERVATION & CO-CREATION

Gardener, writer, teacher, garden designer, philosopher, botanist, and entomologist are some of the words used to describe Gilles Clément and his work. He is something of a Renaissance man of the natural world.

Clément has written and spoken widely on his gardening philosophies. He was interested and passionate about highlighting and deconstructing the way we think about (and the language we use in relation to) the garden and the natural world. Since 1977, he has also been observing and working alongside nature at his own special plot: La Vallée in Creuse, a sparsely populated area of central France. It was here that Clément began to formulate his idea of "the garden in motion": a philosophy he first published in an article in 1985, and later in his 1991 book *Le Jardin en mouvement*.

At La Vallée, Clément crystallizes his notion of the garden in constant flux, and follows his own key principle: to observe more and garden less. Inspired by wasteland, where unmaintained land is quickly claimed by nature, Clément posited that there are dynamic forces at play as soon as we leave nature to it. The gardener can work alongside these forces, utilizing and guiding them rather than attempting to totally dominate them. By its very nature, this type of garden celebrates the constant flux of things; for example, self-seeders and spreaders are encouraged, rather than removed. Clément does not use the term weeding—he prefers to call it "gardening by subtraction."

One objective of gardening this way is to increase biodiversity in soil, water, and air. Another is to garden with an economy of effort, using minimal inputs, no chemical fertilizers or pesticides, and only the most necessary water and tools. Having worked in this way at La Vallée over a number of years, Clément began to use what he had learned in his landscape practice and apply it to other projects, including Parc André Citroën, the Jardins de l'Arche de la Défense, in Paris, and the Henri Matisse Park, in Lille. He also expanded on this thinking with his written works, *The Planetary Garden* and *Manifesto of the Third Landscape*.

Clément has brought a sense of nature into the formal public domain, pushing and evolving our concepts around what landscapes and gardens can be. His work blurs boundaries, and continues a conversation sparked by William Robinson around the relationship between nature and the gardener. As Clément himself states, "The garden produces goods, bears symbols, accompanies dreams. It is accessible to everyone. It promises nothing and gives everything."

ABOVE Looking out from the house, the garden remains a focus even from inside. OPPOSITE Gilles Clément, a great observer of the natural world and its processes. P. 256 The house rests comfortably in the shaggy garden that surrounds it. It was built by Clément over a number of years with local materials.

ABOVE AND OPPOSITE Human elements amidst seas of vegetation—something that speaks to Clément's philosophy of having natural processes involved in the garden. **P. 260** The house appears to grow out of the topography of the site—covered in climbers, the building provides a home to a variety of living things.

A PIONEER OF "RIGHT PLANT, RIGHT PLACE"

Beth Chatto was a horticultural trailblazer. She began work on her garden in 1960, in Essex, the driest part of England—and by embracing these conditions, she created an example of a completely revolutionary garden.

Chatto and her husband Andrew began building their new home on wasteland. Part of the Chatto family fruit farm, the land remained uncultivated due to it being considered too dry in places, and too wet in others. Essex is surprisingly dry, with some parts of the county considered semi-arid. Creating a traditional garden here would undoubtedly be difficult.

But both parties had a deep love of plants and gardening. It was Andrew's research and fascination with the origin of plants that would guide Beth in her choices as she created the garden. Her approach was not to try and fight against the conditions, but to work alongside them, and develop a garden that would thrive in this climate. Her aim was to choose the right plants for the right place.

In 1978, her first book was published: *The Dry Garden.* Here Chatto wrote about high-impact gardens that required little maintenance: gardens filled with plants that could cope with poor soil, hot summers, and dry winters. This was the start of genuine consideration for climate- and context-appropriate planting. Her next book, *The Damp Garden,* followed in 1982, again in direct relation to her experiences of gardening at Beth Chatto Gardens.

Beth's Gravel Garden is probably the most well-known area of the gardens. It began as an experiment: it was never irrigated except by the rain, and had light, free-draining, nutrient-poor soil. Ultimately, the experiment was a success: it is now renowned for its spectacular displays of plants. It seems so obvious now, but choosing plants which could adapt and grow in the specific conditions of your garden was not a familiar concept at the time.

The gardens now contain a diverse array of areas that celebrate the topography and conditions of the land, including a water garden, and a woodland garden with a great variety of shade-loving plants. A scree garden with a selection of alpine and Mediterranean plants is situated on some of the driest, most nutrient-poor soil.

Chatto turned what many would consider "problem" areas into her garden's biggest focus and strength. Her idea of working alongside nature in the garden was well ahead of its time—indeed, her approach would now be considered an example of sustainable and ecological gardening. In the simplest terms, Chatto's ethos boils down to the idea of the right plant, in the right place. Chatto passed away in 2018 at the age of 94; she left a tremendous legacy that still impacts how we approach gardening today.

ABOVE AND P. 264 The Water Garden is a series of ponds full of aquatic and marginal moisture-loving plants. The microclimate here means it is usually a couple of degrees cooler than elsewhere in the garden. **P. 268** The Woodland Garden is a celebration of shade-loving plants—a variety of bulbs, perennials, and shrubs suited to life under the dense canopy of the oaks trees thrives here.

INDEX

Nezu Museum Garden
Tokyo, Japan (pp. 172–183, 228)
Designed by Kengo Kuma
nezu-muse.or.jp
Photos by Haarkon
haarkon.co.uk

El Nido de Quetzalcóatl
Greater Mexico City, Mexico
(pp. 189, 192–203)
Designed by Javier Senosiain
elnidodequetzalcoatl.com
Photos by Anna Dave
annadave.com

Oudolf Field
Somerset, U.K. (pp. 78–83, 88)
Designed by Piet Oudolf
oudolf.com
Photos by Jason Ingram
jasoningram.co.uk

Rain Harvest Home
Temascaltepec, Mexico
(pp. 156–163)
Designed by Robert Hutchison Architecture and JSa Arquitectura
robhutcharch.com
Photos by Rafael Gamo
rafaelgamo.com
(pp. 156, 160, 161)
Laia Rius Sola *@la.laia.rius*
(pp. 158–159)
Cesar Bejar
cesarbejarstudio.com
(pp. 162, 163)

Sissinghurst
Kent, U.K. (pp. 44–53)
Designed by Vita Sackville-West and Harold Nicholson
nationaltrust.org.uk/visit/kent/sissinghurst-castle-garden
Photos by Jo Metson Scott
jometsonscott.com

Sítio Roberto Burle Marx
Rio de Janeiro, Brazil
(pp. 214–225)
Designed by Roberto Burle Marx *burlemarx.com.br*
Photos by Filippo Poli
filippopoli.com

Sussex Farm
East Sussex, U.K.
(pp. 232–237)
Designed by Jinny Blom
jinnyblom.com
Photos by Andrew Montgomery
andrewmontgomery.co.uk
(pp. 232–235, 236 top)
Photos by Nicola Browne
(pp. 236 bottom, 237)

Timba Basalt Quarry Restoration
Gujarat, India (pp. 134–139)
Designed by M/s. Prabhakar B. Bhagwat *landscapeindia.net*
Photos courtesy of M/s. Prabhakar B. Bhagwat

Tokachi Millennium Forest
Shimizu, Japan (pp. 91, 146–155)
Designed by Dan Pearson Studio
danpearsonstudio.com
Photos by Tokachi Millennium Forest, Kiichi Noro, Syogo Oizumi

La Vallée
Creuse, France
(pp. 229 right, 256–263)
Designed by Gilles Clément
gillesclement.com
Photos by Mathieu Génon/Reporterre.net
mathieugenon.net

Wiley At Wildside
Devon, U.K. (pp. 7, 85)
Designed by Keith Wiley
wileyatwildside.com
Photos by Jason Ingram
jasoningram.co.uk

ADDITIONAL IMAGES

Alfio Finocchiaro/Alamy Stock Photo (p. 56), colaimages/Alamy Stock Photo (p. 57), Hervé Lenain/Alamy Stock Photo (p. 59), Hans Blossey/Alamy Stock Photo (p. 89), David Davies/Alamy Stock Photo (p. 113), Peter Schickert/Alamy Stock Photo (p. 114 left), Michael Marquand/Alamy Stock Photo (p. 115), Sergey Kalyakin/Alamy Stock Photo (p. 116), Stephen Roberts Photography/Alamy Stock Photo (p. 117), adoc-photos/Getty Images (p. 185), Amber Rowlands/Liz Davis in her London garden (p. 188), Dan Luca/Alamy Stock Photo (p. 190), Karina Azaretzky/Alamy Stock Photo (p. 191), Jacob Lillis/from his series "Weeds"/*jacoblillis.com* (pp. 229 top left, 230)

TEXT CREDITS

Clément, Gilles. *The Planetary Garden: And Other Writings.* Translated by Sandra Morris. Philadelphia: University of Pennsylvania Press, 2015. (pp. 5, 16)

Gerritsen, Henk. *Henk Gerritsen: Essay on Gardening.* Amsterdam: Architectura & Natura, 2010. (pp. 84, 90)

Gerritsen, Henk. "Maintenance." Philosophy Priona Gardens. Accessed February 7, 2023. *prionatuinen.nl/prionahenk/priona-web/philosophy.html* (pp. 6, 89)

Shintani, Midori. "Tokachi Millennium Forest: The 1,000-Year Garden." Gardens Illustrated. Gardens Illustrated, November 2, 2020. *gardensillustrated.com/gardens/international/tokachi-millennium-forest-dan-pearson* (p. 147)

ACKNOWLEDGEMENTS

With thanks to my parents for opening my eyes to the natural world. A gift like no other.

To my partner Brad Irwin for believing in and encouraging me throughout our relationship and the wonderful women in my life who have and continue to be an inspiration and support—Alison Morris, Amber Rowlands, Clare Smith, Elizabeth Robson, Mavis Watts, Nina Watts, Jo Metson Scott, Karen Stoltzman, Kerry Dales, Lyn Payne, Simone Gooch. And to Jeremy Miller and Paddy Boyce for many years of gardening and growing together.

THE AVANT GARDENS

VISIONARIES AND GARDENS BEYOND WILD EXPECTATIONS

This book was conceived, edited, and designed by **gestalten.**

Edited by **Robert Klanten**
Contributing editor: **John Tebbs**
Editorial support by **Effie Efthymiadi**

Written by **John Tebbs**
Text support by **Dylan McNulty-Holmes**

Editorial Management by **Traci Kim**
Design, layout, and cover by **Joana Sobral**

Photo Editor: **Zoe Paterniani**

Typeface: Bookmania by **Mark Simonson**

Cover images by **Jo Metson Scott**

Printed by Gutenberg Beuys Feindruckerei GmbH, Langenhagen
Made in Germany

Published by gestalten, Berlin 2023
ISBN 978-3-96704-096-8

For more information, and to order books, please visit www.gestalten.com
Bibliographic information published by the Deutsche Nationalbibliothek.

The Deutsche Nationalbibliothek lists this publication in the Deutsche Nationalbibliografie; detailed bibliographic data is available online at www.dnb.de

None of the content in this book was published in exchange for payment by commercial parties or designers; gestalten selected all included work based solely on its artistic merit.

This book was printed on paper certified according to the standards of the FSC®.